The journey of spiritual growth is one of excitement, potential, and purpose. It's one that takes a life-time to experience and even longer to understand. But anyone seeking to take it will at some point ask, "What does it take to grow spiritually?" That question is at the core of my good friend Dharius Daniels's latest book, *Re-Present Jesus*. As he takes us on his own journey of growth, he reveals some unexpected turns. With intelligence, clarity, and candor he takes readers back to the heart of every spiritual journey—back to Jesus. And he helps us discover the purpose, potential, and excitement of what God wants us all to experience.

—ED YOUNG
PASTOR, FELLOWSHIP CHURCH
AUTHOR, *YOU: THE JOURNEY TO THE CENTER OF YOUR WORTH*

Every so often God sends us men and women with a divine message that causes us to reshape, refocus, and redefine our relationship with Him. I believe that He has sent my friend Pastor Dharius Daniels to do just that. So many times we define our Christian walk by how morally upright we are or how many rules we adhere to that we miss the big picture of simply being more like Christ. In his book *Re-Present Jesus* Pastor Daniels challenges us all to reevaluate our walk with Christ, and to ask ourselves at the end of the day, "Did I become more like Jesus today?"

—SHERYL BRADY
PASTOR, THE POTTER'S HOUSE OF NORTH DALLAS
AUTHOR, *YOU HAVE IT IN YOU!*

We are living in an hour of a major cultural shift. Regrettably in the West, that shift is away from godliness. There is, however, in the midst of this shift being raised up a remnant of radical voices that are determined to give power to the purpose and presence of the life-changing gospel of Jesus Christ. One such voice is that of Dharius Daniels. In his book *Re-Present Jesus* Dharius challenges us to look clearly at what it *really* means to submit our lives and follow Christ. His words prompt us to put feet to our faith, and to not only ascribe to being hearers of the Word, but also doers as well. I believe this is a must-read for not only every serious biblical scholar and student, but also for those who have decided to follow the Lord. While it is not in vogue, a hymn from my youth comes to mind, *"I have decided to follow Jesus; No turning back, no turning back."* This book is not for the faint of heart. It is challenging, cutting edge, relevant, and revolutionary, and I believe that it has come into the kingdom for such a time as this.

—Dr. Donald Hilliard Jr.
Lead pastor, Cathedral International
Affiliate associate professor, Drew
Theological Seminary

Being that Jesus Christ is the most googled personality on the Internet, you would think that we would have a great understanding of who He is. Unfortunately many of us have been presented a one-dimensional Jesus without discovering the depth of His humanity and divinity. Like Simeon who was compelled to carry the cross of Christ, my friend Dharius Daniels has compelled us to get under the cross of cultural construction to deconstruct our misconceptions and represent a Christ who is fully known. Many people have been presented a rigid Jesus who's ready to pounce on our moral miscues, but Pastor Dharius Daniels represents a Jesus who wants a relationship with us to redeem our humanity. This book will reintroduce Jesus to a people who may be cautious of religion but longing for relationship with the Son of God.

—Dr. Stacy Spencer
Lead pastor, New Direction Christian Church

Dharius Daniels reminds me what spiritual transformation is all about. His new book, *Re-Present Jesus,* liberates us with the truth of what it means to submit to God out of passionate gratitude, our only response to such amazing grace. As Dharius draws us back to the truth of Christ's character, we're not only set free but also inspired to become more like Jesus!

—Chris Hodges
Senior pastor, Church of the Highlands
Author of *Fresh Air* and *Four Cups*

This book is a premier "kingdom culture" book! In this work my mentor, Dharius Daniels, correctly communicates that much of what has been taught about Christianity has been either incorrect or incomplete. In these pages lie the realignment of God's intent as it pertains to Christ in our culture. Jesus has not been presented properly, and this book shows us how to re-present Him. Get ready to be challenged, get ready to be changed, get ready to become more like Jesus.

—Tye Tribbet
Two-time Grammy Award–winning
gospel artist

RePRESENT

JESUS

DHARIUS DANIELS

Passio

Most CHARISMA HOUSE BOOK GROUP products are available at special quantity discounts for bulk purchase for sales promotions, premiums, fund–raising, and educational needs. For details, write Charisma House Book Group, 600 Rinehart Road, Lake Mary, Florida 32746, or telephone (407) 333–0600.

RE-PRESENT JESUS by Dharius Daniels
Published by Passio
Charisma Media/Charisma House Book Group
600 Rinehart Road
Lake Mary, Florida 32746
www.charismahouse.com

Unless otherwise noted, all Scripture quotations are from the Holy Bible, New International Version®, NIV®. Copyright © 1973, 1978, 1984, 2011 by Biblica, Inc.™ Used by permission of Zondervan. All rights reserved worldwide. www .zondervan.com The "NIV" and "New International Version" are trademarks registered in the United States Patent and Trademark Office by Biblica, Inc.™

Scripture quotations marked KJV are from the King James Version of the Bible.

Scripture quotations marked NAS are from the New American Standard Bible, copyright © 1960, 1962, 1963, 1968, 1971, 1972, 1973, 1975, 1977, 1995 by The Lockman Foundation. Used by permission. (www.Lockman.org)

Cover design by Lisa Rae Cox and Justin Evans
Design Director: Justin Evans

Visit the author's website at www.dhariusdaniels.com.

Library of Congress Control Number: 2014908845
International Standard Book Number: 978-1-62136-585-3
E-book ISBN: 978-1-62136-586-0

First edition

14 15 16 17 18 — 9 8 7 6 5 4 3 2 1
Printed in the United States of America

CONTENTS

ACKNOWLEDGMENTS

With special thanks:

To my amazing wife, Shameka Daniels, whose love and support helped make this book possible.

To my two sons, Seth and Gabriel, who bring me such joy and balance.

To my father, Timothy Daniels, who raised me to believe I could do anything.

To the entire Kingdom Church family who first received the Re-Present message with openness and humility.

To Lonnell Williams, Shaun Saunders, and Marc Jeffrey for your dedication, coordination, and guidance.

To the hosts of pastors, mentors, and friends who coach and support me.

To the Charisma House family for believing in and taking a chance on this message.

INTRODUCTION

HAVE YOU EVER been misrepresented? Strictly speaking, have your words ever been taken out of context, your activities misunderstood, or your associations judged? If so, you will probably concur that it can be a very frustrating experience. Although we are aware we cannot control other people's perceptions of us, we would like for their opinions to be based on who we really are and what we really say. Most of us are not expecting to be represented perfectly, but we do desire to be represented properly. When we aren't, it can be extremely upsetting.

If being misrepresented is upsetting for us, I can only imagine what it feels like to God. Unfortunately God has to deal with it much more than we do. As a matter of fact, those who claim to know Him best often misrepresent Him most.

ARE WE LIKE JESUS?

I came across a recent survey commissioned by the Fermi Project and conducted by the Barna Group that corroborates this claim. One aspect of the survey researched the top words non-Christians use to describe Christians. The most used descriptors were such words as *judgmental, insensitive, homophobic,* and *hypocritical.*[1]

My concern with this data is not that Christians are unpopular; I am aware surveys can be highly skewed and that the goal of our faith is not to win a popularity contest. Rather, my issue with this data is that many of the words used to describe Christians do not describe Jesus.

It suggests that in many instances, Christians are not like Christ. It's like the quote Gandhi is credited with saying: "I like your Christ but I do not like your Christians. Your Christians are so unlike your Christ."[2]

This is a huge problem and a mirror that reveals a much larger issue: Christians have greatly misunderstood what it means to be one. The governing assumption seems to be that a Christian is one who has received Jesus instead of one who follows Him. In other words, the word *Christian* is understood to mean a person who *likes Jesus* as opposed to one who is *like Jesus*. And if this is our understanding of Christianity, then it will inevitably affect our understanding of spiritual growth.

I know this from personal experience. Earlier in my life I associated the terms *spiritual growth* and *godliness* with morality and spiritual disciplines. I erroneously assumed that if my behavior was moral and I engaged in spiritual disciplines, that would lead to spiritual growth. I assumed if I was praying, studying Scripture, and living morally, I was growing. As a result, I spent a large part of my spiritual journey pursuing the equivalent of spiritual face-lifts when what I actually needed was a heart transplant. I was converted, pious, moral, and disciplined, but I completely misunderstood what it means to grow spiritually.

But then some time ago, as I was studying the Scriptures, I began to see an interesting and recurring theme that radically altered my perspective. I noticed passages such as these:

> For those God foreknew he also predestined *to be conformed to the image of his Son*, that he might be the firstborn among many brothers and sisters.
> —ROMANS 8:29, EMPHASIS ADDED

> My dear children, for whom I am again in the pains of childbirth *until Christ is formed in you*.
> —GALATIANS 4:19, EMPHASIS ADDED

After encountering several passages similar to these, I had an epiphany. Spiritual growth isn't necessarily about doing more; it's about becoming more like Jesus!

Prayer is important, but God's ultimate goal is not to get us to pray more. Morality is essential, but God's ultimate goal is not just to get us to do more moral things. God's priority is to make us like Jesus. Godliness and spiritual growth can really be described in one Word: *Jesus*. In other words, Jesus is more than a savior; He is an example. He is the ultimate expression of what it means to live a godly life.

This perspective rocked my spiritual world. I realized I needed to become like Christ. However, being a pragmatist, I could not stop there. I had to ask myself the question, "What is Jesus Christ like?" Amazingly and disturbingly I could only provide generic, nonspecific answers. I was the pastor of a large congregation, had Ivy League seminary training, and had been a Christian as long as I could remember, but I didn't really know what Jesus was like. I had read, heard, and preached about His resurrection, His miracles, His blood, His sacrifice, and His ministry, but I didn't know much about His character.

I realized there was an image of Jesus in my mind that was possibly inconsistent with the image of Jesus in the

Scriptures. Therefore, I needed to be *re-presented* with the Jesus of the Scriptures so that I could properly represent *that* Jesus in my life. That led me on a journey to study the Gospels and learn as much as I could about the character of Christ so I could ask the Holy Spirit to cultivate those traits in my character.

This book contains what I discovered on my journey. It is my attempt to capture twelve core aspects of who Jesus is and re-present them to you, so that you too can experience the life change that comes from living like Jesus lived. First of all, we will explore Jesus's chief character trait, which is love. When I say love, trust me, it is not what you may think! This chapter will clarify what Jesus actually means when He instructs us to love others, including our enemies.

You may be surprised to discover that Jesus isn't giving us instruction on how to feel but rather challenging us to expand our understanding of love beyond simple affection to how we treat others. In other words, this chapter teaches that biblical love isn't simply about affection; it's about activity. When Jesus instructs us to love others, He isn't simply concerned with how we feel about them but rather how we treat them. Jesus isn't saying feel something; He is saying do something.

Next, in chapter 2 we will address the importance and significance of truth. Jesus modeled a life of truth and communicated that it sets us free. It's one thing to tell the truth; it is another thing to live in it. In this chapter we will learn how to experience freedom from facades and live truthfully, authentically, and freely. An associate of mine often says, "Be real, because being fake is exhausting." Agreed! After we address the significance of truth, this chapter will also coach you on how to share some "hard truths" with others. Jesus had to have some hard conversations. So will we.

In chapter 3 we will discover how Jesus is the epitome and embodiment of grace. Grace is a challenging subject. We all love to receive it but struggle to give it. This chapter will expand our understanding of how Jesus sees grace, and consequently may reveal that we aren't as grace-full as we may think. However, we do reap what we sow. Therefore we should learn to walk with grace because one day we may fall and be in need of it.

Chapter 4 is one of my favorites. It focuses on wisdom. As a pastor, I am exposed to a plethora of words that people use to describe Jesus. Unfortunately *wise* is rarely one of them. However, Luke 2:52 clearly claims that Jesus grew in wisdom, and if we were to examine His activity with individuals throughout the Gospels, it would corroborate that claim. Jesus wasn't just righteous; He was also wise. Consequently, if we are going to follow in His footsteps we must grasp that godliness isn't just living morally; it is also living wisely. This chapter will help you do that. Others benefit from your gifts; you benefit from your wisdom. When wisdom isn't emphasized we end up being good people but not wise ones, and in order to properly represent Jesus we need both.

Chapter 5 is another one of my favorites (I have a lot of favorites). It is titled "Jesus and the S-Word." It's about...well, you just have to read that one.

In Chapter 6 we examine how Jesus's life was the ultimate expression of generosity. This chapter will teach us the importance of modeling generosity. It will teach how generosity is one of the ways we can avoid unintentional idolatry and ensure that Jesus is Lord of all. This chapter acknowledges the reality of the rise of gimmicks when it comes to giving in contemporary Christianity. However, it has been said that we don't correct wrong teaching with nonteaching; we correct wrong teaching with right teaching. This chapter reminds us of what generosity looks like when it is done the "Jesus way."

Chapter 7 is probably one of the most important chapters in the book. It re-presents the nature and importance of spiritual disciplines. In this chapter I contend that what exercise is to an athlete, spiritual discipline is to the Christian. There is no way we can do what Jesus did in public without doing what Jesus did in private. You don't end up like Jesus by accident. This chapter exposes what some of Jesus's disciplines were and gives us encouragement and instruction on how to implement them in our own lives.

Chapter 8 re-presents to us the way Jesus managed relationships. Your greatest pleasure and pain will often come from the same place: your relationships. However, Jesus provided an amazing and effective model for managing them, and this chapter exposes it and instructs us on how to follow it. Jesus had a "place" for everyone in His life. He never apologized for not giving someone a place in His life He was not comfortable with them being in. This chapter will help you learn how to put people in their place.

Chapter 9 explores one of Jesus's most effective tools: His words. Jesus was constantly confronted with cynics and critics who would attempt to trap Him. However, He avoided unnecessary inconvenience in His life because He used His words wisely and responsibly. His words not only benefited Him; they also benefited others. Grace, love, and hope were often transported into people's lives through the vehicle of words. This chapter will equip you with the insight you need to emulate Jesus in this area so that your words bless your life and the lives of others.

Chapter 10 is one of the most challenging and rewarding chapters in the book. This chapter is titled "Jesus and Forgiveness." Forgiveness is one of the most important concepts in Christianity. Our faith rests in the reality that we have experienced forgiveness. However, in my experience I have discovered it is one of the subjects about which people are the most confused. This subject is too essential for anyone to be unclear. In this chapter we clearly and simply explain what forgiveness is, what it isn't, how Jesus modeled it, and how we can practice it. This chapter will help release you from the paralyzing pain of the past and push you into the next chapter of God's story for your life.

Chapter 11 addresses another essential yet confusing topic—the subject of faith. In this chapter you will learn how Jesus views faith and consequently how we should view it. You will discover that faith doesn't alter the will of God; it accomplishes it. It is not a leash that we can wrap around God's neck to lead Him to our will. Rather, faith is what God uses to lead us into His will. This chapter will explore what faith is. Faith is not optimism; it produces optimism, but it shouldn't be confused with or limited to optimism. Also, this chapter will offer biblical and proven insight on how to grow your faith. Growing our faith isn't always about our faith getting bigger. Jesus said that we could move mountains with faith the size of mustard seeds. Growing our faith is about our faith getting broader.

Finally, chapter 12 addresses the X factor that empowers us to become like Jesus—the Holy Spirit. In this chapter you will learn that Jesus lived a life of complete reliance on the presence and power of the Holy Spirit. If Jesus had to rely on the Holy Spirit to be Jesus then it goes without saying that we have to rely on Him as well to be like Jesus. Together, we explore the biblical truth that the Holy Spirit is not some*thing* but rather He is some*one*, and this Someone wants to help us become like *the* One, Jesus Christ.

I'm going to level with you: this material changed my life. It released me from the spiritual hamster wheel and escorted me into the experience of joy, peace, and fulfillment I had previously read about in the Scriptures but until recently had never experienced for myself.

I want that kind of experience for you. And it's not just me who wants it—God wants it for you too. He wants to unlock, unearth, and unleash the potential inside you, but here's the reality: it only comes through intentional Christlike growth. I pray this book serves as a map that directs you to the next level in your spiritual life: becoming more like Jesus.

So, are you ready to learn about Jesus all over again? Get ready to represent! Get ready...set...*grow!*

Chapter 1

JESUS and LOVE

I pray that you will understand the words of Jesus, "Love one another as I have loved you." Ask your-self "How has He loved me? Do I really love others in the same way?" Unless this love is among us, we can kill ourselves with work and it will only be work, not love. Work without love is slavery.[1]
—MOTHER TERESA

I F I WERE to ask you, "Do you love Jesus," what would you say? It's a simple question, and I imagine many of you reading this book would answer with an impassioned and unequivocal yes! You may even wonder why I would ask such an unnecessary question. Obviously you love Jesus; otherwise you wouldn't be reading this book, right? But before you throw this book to the side or gift it to an "unsaved family member," slow down for a moment. Think about what I am asking you and try not to jump to conclusions. Do you, (insert your name), truly love Jesus—not your church or your denomination, not your political position or theological conviction—but Jesus.

Just Jesus.

Please grant me the personal privilege of asking another question: "How do you know you love Him and do you think Jesus would agree with you?" OK, that was two. And I have one more: What would you say if I told you that loving Christ means more than "loving Christ" as an emotional exercise, but also includes loving like Christ? This is the question at the heart of this chapter.

Unfortunately, contemporary notions have reduced love to feelings. Although love affects our feelings, impacts our feelings, and at times intensifies our feelings, it should not be viewed as simply a feeling. The kind of love we want and God deserves is demonstrable love. It is visible love. This is the type of love God has shown us. It's the type of love that describes Jesus, and it's the type of love that should describe those who follow Him.

One of the most dominant character traits that describes Jesus is love. He frequently taught on it, prioritized it, told parables about it, and modeled it. However, when the topic of love comes up in books like this, most of us stop paying attention. We assume we know all there is to know about Jesus and love because we're Bible-toting, bumper-sticker-sporting, cross-wearing Christians.

But I plead with you not to jump to theological conclusions about this. Throw away every assumption. Open your mind to the possibility that your files on any subject can be updated. Walk with me down every street, and do not skip over the scriptures you already know. If you do skip along on this, you may miss the most essential ingredient in re-presenting Christ: the Jesus kind of love. Jesus models a type of love that is different from and— dare I say—transcends the fleeting, temperamental, elusive notion of love many live with. Christ's love is not lyrical or passive. It's not predicated on conditions or ultimatums. Instead, His love—demonstrated through the life He lived on earth—is grounded in an unadulterated commitment to the will of God. His love didn't hang on the vacillating hinges of His feelings. It proved itself by walking the walk and talking the talk.

That, my friends, is what this chapter is about: love on another level.

Let's discover what this love is all about.

A JESUS KIND OF LOVE

> A new command I give you: Love one another. As I have loved you, so you must love one another. By this everyone will know that you are my disciples, if you love one another.
>
> —JOHN 13:34–35

Jesus makes a bold statement in John 13:34–35. He announces to us that the way the world will know we are His followers is not by the crosses around our necks, our attendance at worship services, or the Bibles we throw in the back windows of our cars. The way the world will know us to be His followers is by our love.

But why does Jesus begin His commentary with "a new commandment"? What is at stake in this moment that requires Jesus to present a new way of understanding the law?

As you may recall, Jesus is not talking to Christians here. He's talking to Jews who are well aware of the commandments of God. Christians mainly focus on the Decalogue, also known as the Ten Commandments, but

Moses actually received 613 commandments from God on Mount Sinai. Jews were not naïve to this. So when Jesus said, "A new commandment I give," their ears perked up. He's speaking their language, and they're waiting to see what He's going to say next.

He opens His expository sermon with these words: "Love one another *as I have loved you*." Pause. Slow down. Take that in for a minute. Loving one another is a general expectation. It's something every person of religious conviction should already know to do. But when Jesus says "as I have loved you," He launches into unfamiliar territory. He challenges His listeners to think about the way He has modeled love—and then He commands them to mirror that kind of love to everyone else.

In no uncertain terms Jesus argues that all Christians should demonstrate to their neighbors the kind of love they have received from their Savior. *As I have loved you, love them.* In other words, *reciprocate love to Me by doing this to everyone else.*

In these two verses Jesus gives what I call a Christocentric hermeneutic. The word *hermeneutic* refers to a chosen method of interpreting Scripture. A Christocentric hermeneutic, then, places Jesus's life and teachings at the center of biblical interpretation.

If we are going to re-present Christ in the world, we must develop a Christocentric hermeneutic. That means instead of asking, "What does the Bible say?" or "What do I think I should do?" we are now challenged to ask: "How did Jesus respond?" "How did Jesus love?" "How did Jesus behave?" "How did Jesus react?" This is a Christocentric hermeneutic. Scripture is filled with examples of Jesus modeling this method for us.

One example is found in Luke 24, when Jesus is on the road to Emmaus. By this point He has already resurrected, and after bumping into two of His disciples on the road, He opens up the Scriptures to them, answering all their questions about what had happened with the Crucifixion event. After Jesus shares a meal with them and then disappears from their sight after the breaking of bread, the two disciples ask each other, "Were not our hearts burning within us while he talked with us on the road and opened the Scriptures to us?" (Luke 24:32).

What is happening here? Why did they make this statement?

Jesus did not literally open a book to explain the Scriptures to them, but He did show His disciples how the book had always alluded to Him. He brought Hebrews 10:7 to life: "Lo, I come (in the volume of the book it is written of me)" (KJV). He showed them how Abraham represents Christ, since Abraham left his country and Christ had to leave His. He showed them how Isaac represents Christ insofar as Isaac had to carry his own wood to give up his own life at the request of his father, and Christ had to do the same. It was a Christocentric hermeneutic. By opening the Scriptures in fresh ways, Jesus proved to these disciples (and He does the same for us now) that all scripture written in the Book testifies of Him—even popular scriptures such as John 3:16.

A Refusal to Condemn

John 3:16 has been dubbed the most famous Bible verse ever, and for good reason. In it are the central themes of Christianity—God's gift of salvation, eternal life, and faith—all wrapped around one major ribbon in verb form: *love.*

The verse begins telling the story about salvation, and most of us know it by memory. The problem is, we don't often think about what comes after it. It is John 3:17 that sets the parameters for John 3:16. Consider the verses:

> For God so loved the world that he gave his one and only Son, that whoever believes in him shall not perish but have eternal life. For God did not send his Son into the world to condemn the world, but to save the world through him.

There you have it. Once again Jesus is found doing something His followers are not doing. Christ came to save—He did not come to condemn—whereas Christians tend to condemn but use condemnation as bait toward salvation. Jesus came to give, but Christians often take. His was a ministry of reconciliation; ours is often a ministry of judgment. It's the craziest marketing strategy in the world—the idea that *guilting* people into salvation will cause them to love God more.

Speaking of which, I'll never forget a Facebook post I saw last November. It was Thanksgiving night, and many people in the photo were gathered around a particular store in preparation for Black Friday. Like every year, lines were wrapped around the building for hours as consumers hoped to catch a bargain.

But the picture wasn't the issue. The crowd wasn't the issue. The comments below the photo are what grabbed my attention.

Most responders were shocked to see the magnitude

of people tenting out. Others identified where they had been standing in line. And of course, there was one lovely comment made by a fellow Christian that read, "If people would line up like this and come to the house of God, the world wouldn't be in the shape it's in."

This person must not have read John 3:17. Or if she read it, she didn't allow it to transform her theology. She was a "do not" Christian—do not cuss, do not fuss, do not go, do not stay. Her language was filled with condemnation and self-righteousness. What's worse, I wonder if she actually thought her comment would make some reader ask, "What, then, must I do to be saved?"

Jesus says in John 3:17, "I didn't come for that." He didn't come to drown people in the pool of sin—He came to save people from their sins! He didn't come so His followers could build a glass house and throw rocks at unbelievers; rather, He came as a lifeguard for humanity with one goal: to rescue, redeem, and restore us back to Himself.

Romans 5:8 frames it this way: "But God demonstrates his own love for us in this: while we were still sinners, Christ died for us." This divine love act in the form of death on the cross was an undeniable demonstration of God's love. But even more significant than the fact that He died is *when* He died. The "when" matters here just as much as the "how" mattered in the beginning of this chapter.

Jesus died for us *while we were yet sinners*. Before our conduct deserved it, He died. Before our actions could appreciate it, He died. In the same way that God's love for us was not based on conduct, our love for others must not be based on conduct. This was the love Jesus displayed for a people who did not even accept Him. His love was unflinching. His love was unconditional. His love was not predicated on reciprocity. His love was rooted in obedience to the Father. This is agape love.

AN EXPANDED CONCEPT

One of them, an expert in the law, tested him with this question: "Teacher, which is the greatest commandment in the Law?"

Jesus replied: "'Love the Lord your God with all your heart and with all your soul and with all your mind.' This is the first and greatest commandment. And the second is like it: 'Love your neighbor as yourself.' All the Law and the Prophets hang on these two commandments."

—MATTHEW 22:35–40

In the English language, we have only one word for *love*. So when I say "I love my children" or "I love my wife" or "I love my boss," you know what I mean. Certainly I do not love my wife the same way I love my boss. I'm sure you do not love your boss the same way you love your children either. In Greek (the language in which the New Testament was written) there are several different words for love. They had words to describe love for family, love for friends, and love for lovers. So depending on the person, you would use one word or another to describe your love for them.

Jesus, however, was very strategic when it came to His word usage for love. The word He frequently used to describe it wasn't the kind of love we would have for family, friends, or spouses. More often than not, He used another word—*agape*.

Rarely used in extrabiblical Greek, agape is an unselfish, unconditional, unconquerable benevolence. There is nothing you can do to conquer it and nothing you can do to stop it. It is a decision to seek the highest good for others and to seek to do what is in a person's best interest, whether they reciprocate that love or not.

The good news about agape love is that it is not predicated on feelings. It is a love of the will—a decision. Therefore, whenever Jesus tells us to love like He loved, He isn't telling us to feel a certain thing. Feelings can be managed, but they can't be controlled or commanded.

Let's try it.

Get happy. No, really—get happy. Right now, stop what you are doing and get happy. I'll wait.

It's not happening, is it? You can smile and you can act out happiness, but you can't command feelings of happiness.

I think this distinction is incredibly important. I'm not saying love doesn't stir up affection or stimulate feelings. I'm saying we can't reduce biblical love—the Jesus type of love—to the arena of feelings. Jesus modeled and expects more than feelings. Therefore, when He commands us to love, He is not telling us to feel for others the way we feel for our friends. Instead, He is calling us to demonstrate a Jesus kind of love for them.

Jesus is the template that shows us how to love the Christian way. But often we Christians have a habit of taking the stuff we want and throwing away the verses we don't want. When that seed of selective gospel grows, it births a Christianity that is opposite the Christ who bears its name.

There is a difference between a love that obeys and a love that enslaves. Enslaved love is subjective and conditional. It is only committed to something insofar as its participants hold up their end of the bargain. Agape love, however, does not look for reciprocity. It does not expect 50/50. Instead, it makes a decision to love God by treating all persons the same way Christ would treat them.

This is the essence of what Jesus was speaking about in Matthew 22. After Jesus was asked a trick question, He responded to the Pharisees in two ways. First, He said to love God with all of your heart, soul, and mind. Loving God is the priority. What we do horizontally flows from our relationships vertically. Loving God with all of our souls means loving God unselfishly. This kind of love is impossible without Christ. In fact, that's what makes our love so distinguishable. Human beings without Christ cannot fathom this phenomenon. Christ instructs and empowers us to do it.

Jesus then continues, "The second commandment is like it: 'Love your neighbor as yourself.' All the Law and the Prophets hang on these two commandments" (vv. 39–40). We already know that Jesus has modeled this love, but now He is adding another challenge to the love equation. When you love God and love your neighbor as yourself, Jesus says every other commandment will relate to these two. So we don't have to be told not to cheat, lie, or talk behind others' backs. If you love your neighbor as yourself, you won't steal from them, cheat them, or bring them harm anyway.

IT'S ALL ABOUT THE FRUIT

From time to time we may wonder how this works in our everyday lives, and Paul paints a practical picture for us in 1 Corinthians 13. Paul's audience in Corinth was a well-meaning, sincere, yet misguided group of Christians. The congregation was extremely blessed, but at the same time, they were relationally dysfunctional. I mean, *really*. They found every reason to argue—who was baptizing whom, who should speak when, and who should not speak at all—and their worship gatherings were full of charismatic competitions. Yes, they loved God, but they couldn't get along with one another. Sound familiar?

For this reason, Paul writes them a letter to bring guidance on how they ought to relate to one another. He ends 1 Corinthians 12 by saying, "Let me show you a more excellent way," and begins 1 Corinthians 13 with this commentary on agape love:

> If I speak in the tongues of men or of angels, but do not have love, I am only a resounding gong or a clanging cymbal. If I have the gift of prophecy and can fathom all mysteries and all knowledge, and if I have a faith that can move mountains, but do not have love, I am nothing. If I give all I possess to the poor and give over my body to hardship that I may boast, but do not have love, I gain nothing.
>
> Love is patient, love is kind. It does not envy, it does not boast, it is not proud. It does not dishonor others, it is not self-seeking, it is not easily angered, it keeps no record of wrongs. Love does not delight in evil but rejoices with the truth. It

always protects, always trusts, always hopes, always perseveres.

Love never fails. But where there are prophecies, they will cease; where there are tongues, they will be stilled; where there is knowledge, it will pass away. For we know in part and we prophesy in part, but when completeness comes, what is in part disappears. When I was a child, I talked like a child, I thought like a child, I reasoned like a child. When I became a man, I put the ways of childhood behind me.

—1 CORINTHIANS 13:1–11

If we remember Paul's audience, we can see how every verse here speaks to relational dysfunction. Paul draws on Jesus's example and spells out how love should look, behave, think, and respond. By the end of his letter, he tells the church to put away childish behaviors and love the way Jesus Christ has empowered us to love. Throughout each line of this passage, Paul exalts fruit over gift.

Revisit the verses for a moment. First, Paul mentions the gift of tongues, the gift of prophecy, the gift of faith, and the gift of generosity. Isn't it crazy—someone can burn his or her own body and still amount to nothing without love? Paul uses these examples of deeds to deconstruct the norm.

We're just like the norm. We think we have to do something in order to prove our love loyalties. We think we have to wear a certain kind of robe or sing in the choir every first and third Sunday. But none of these deeds prove love to God. They may prove your love to the church or to your own reputation. But Paul is challenging Corinth to live out what Jesus has already lived out.

Our deeds are only a consequence of our obedience. To love God with your whole heart requires that you focus on the fruit rather than obsessing about the gift. We must focus more on God than on man and concentrate more on our faith than we do our feelings. Christlikeness—not the flaunting of one's talents—is the goal.

In verse 4 Paul spells out what agape is. Agape is patient and kind. It does not envy, and it does not boast. Instead, it prays God will save the lost but does not rush the saving process due to impatience. Godly love remembers how long it took us to get saved and commits to helping others grow over time. Christ's love is not proud, and it does not dishonor others. So when dining at a local diner, we should not disparage the server by talking to her in any kind of negative or condescending way. Everyone deserves respect and embrace. Love is not self-seeking, and it is not easily angered. In practical terms it doesn't listen to others just so others can listen back. Love doesn't fly off the handle and pierce people with venomous phrases. Instead, it thinks before it speaks, and it gives before it takes.

Agape does not keep a record of wrongs, and it does not delight in evil but rejoices with the truth. This means you should not hold your spouse hostage by refusing to forgive them years after they've asked you to forgive them for an infraction. If they apologized for their wrongdoing, let it go! In the same way, do not provoke your children by bringing up their pasts. Instead, protect, trust, hope, and persevere. The love of God covers, invests, and points toward a better future.

These are the characteristic traits of God's love, but remember to keep all of this in context. Paul is speaking about how others will know we are followers of Christ. He wants to answer the questions, "How will outsiders notice something about us is different? How will our witness be strengthened by our interactions with one another?" The quick answer: by our commitment to love out loud! The long answer: by our steadfast resolve to look to Jesus for instruction and by our willingness to fellowship with one another.

When we demonstrate the heart of God, we exemplify agape. When our love language matches Christ's unconditional sacrifice, we exemplify agape. As Christ has loved us, so must we also love one another. Love is where we must start. Love is where we must end.

Chapter 2

JESUS and TRUTH

The truth that makes men free is for the most part the truth which men prefer not to hear.[1]
—HERBERT AGAR

GEORGE ORWELL IS noted as saying, "In a time of universal deceit, telling the truth is a revolutionary act." I have to admit that I agree with Orwell's assessment. Truthfulness is revolutionary. It is revolutionary because deceit has become the preferred method of being. Our world in general, and this nation in particular, is fascinated with fantasy. We buy houses we can't afford, fraternize with people we don't like, and attend parties dressed in outfits we plan to return in order to be accepted by strangers who barely know our names. The success of reality TV shows that aren't depicting reality and of billion-dollar entertainment industries reveals a fatal flaw about the human condition: we are infatuated with fiction. Deception is a fiction narrative based on a true story prompted by a decision to substitute reality for idealism. In other words, we don't keep it real.

In my opinion it all began in the Garden of Eden. The serpent deceived Eve into eating the forbidden fruit in order to become someone other than her true self. From that moment on, the world entered into a downward spiral of disarray and perpetual defeat where deception became interwoven into the fabric of our lives. Deception tricked Abraham into lying about his wife, Sarah. Deception convinced Jacob to steal his brother's birthright. Deception caused Achan to partake in forbidden things. Deception comes from the adversary, and if given permission, he will use everything in his arsenal to deceive us.

God seems to be very patient with imperfection, but He seems less tolerant of deception. Proverbs 6:17–19 outlines six things the Lord hates, and deception is mentioned twice. A lying tongue and a heart that devises wicked plans are both deceptive vices. I believe our Lord loathes deception because lying is the devil's native language. John 8:44 tells us in plain English that the devil is the father of lies. He is the progenitor of deception. The devil has a PhD in L-I-E, and his goal is to blind minds and deceive hearts. If the enemy can persuade you to be untruthful due to fear, perception, image, or selfishness, he can cause you to dishonor God. Where truth is distorted, honor is aborted.

And this is the world Jesus enters as a revolutionary of truth to break the curse of deceit. Throughout His entire life, we see the power of truth. Where truth is not present, Christlike character is absent. If you are serious about re-presenting Jesus accurately, then you must become a person of truth.

The Gospels clearly reveal that truth was a virtue Jesus

prioritized in His own life and ministry. John 1:14 says Jesus was "full of grace and truth" (KJV). Later Jesus self-identifies as "the way, the truth, and the life" (John 14:6, KJV). Jesus blesses His followers in John 8 with these words: "If you hold to my teaching, you are really my disciples. Then you will know the truth, and the truth will set you free" (vv. 31–32). Again we see the connection between God's truth and God's Word. But also we see the freedom of His truth. Jesus says, in essence, "My truth brings life and liberty. If you get to know Me, you will get to know boundless and bountiful truth. But until you know the truth—Me—you cannot experience, walk in, or tell the truth."

Jesus says in John 8, "The truth shall set you free." The entire chapter is a battle over truth—Jesus and the Pharisees on two sides of the same fence. On the left, you have Jesus on the side of spirit and truth. On the right, you have the Pharisees on the side of law and logic. In the first scene (vv. 1–11) they bring a woman to Jesus who was caught in the act of adultery (an episode we will unpack further in the next chapter). The teachers of the law are so imprisoned by religious ideology that they cannot see the object of their theology. Jesus came to fulfill the law, not to abolish it, but they don't get it. So they challenge Him. They question His authority. They question His testimony. Back and forth they dispute and dispute, until Jesus finally says, "If you knew me, you would know my Father also" (v. 19). You would think these words settle the dispute, but they don't, because we read, "They [still] did not understand" (v. 27).

Here we have a past problem that has metastasized into a present-day plague. Like the Pharisees, many

17

churches and Christians alike promote a truth about Christ inconsistent with the Father's truth about Christ. Like the Pharisees, we are often taken aback when Christ shows up, because He does not look or sound like what we expected. The Pharisees were stuck on presuppositions and outdated prescriptions. Jesus was standing directly in front of them, and still they couldn't see Him.

How many of us struggle with this same bifocal conflict of truth and lie? The Pharisees knew the law but they couldn't see the Lord because their minds were blinded by deception. But Jesus walks in truth and desperately desires those of us who follow Him to live in it as well— to see Him truly. And in order to do so, we must answer a basic question.

WHAT IS TRUTH?

To tackle this basic question, I want to begin by explaining what truth is *not*. First of all, divine truth is not synonymous with human opinion. In other words, truth is not truth because your mother did it this way. Truth is not truth because of traditional patterns or cultural habits. Truth is not rooted in logic, because logic is not an authority on spiritual matters. I am not saying truth isn't logical; I am simply saying there are times when it transcends logic.

Degrees do not legitimate truth. Gray hair does not indicate truth. Our opinion of something or someone does not always reflect truth accurately. No matter how long a nation has existed, governing leaders and founding fathers are still human beings, which means our conclusions are restricted to a subjective human experience unless we base those conclusions on something higher than ourselves. Real truth extends beyond us, reaches over us, and is never decided by us.

So, what is truth? Jesus clearly answers this question in a prayer recorded in John 17. He says to the Father, "Sanctify them by the truth; your word is truth" (v. 17). This is the barometer by which Christ measures truthfulness: the Word. All truth comes from the Word.

I am not saying truth is only found in Scripture. I am saying, however, that if anything contradicts Scripture, then it isn't true. If our opinion lines up with the Word of God, then it's true. If it doesn't, then it's a lie. It's as simple as that. If our feelings line up with the Word of God, then they're true. If they don't, then they aren't. Our feelings may be real but that doesn't mean they're true. God is the only one with perfect feelings. Therefore, God always feels what should be felt, and whatever He feels is always right. Our feelings are not perfect and they can't be the source we use to determine what's true or the compass we use to direct our lives.

I often encounter individuals who assume passion and intensity of feeling is an accurate indicator of truth. They assume they wouldn't feel so strongly about something if it weren't real. How many times has that been said prior to making a detrimental decision about marriage, business, or life?

Our feelings are important and vital. However, they cannot always be trusted. The Word of God is the only truth you can trust. It is the Supreme Court to which we bring every case in question. It is the arbitrator of ideas. It is the decipherer of all disputes. When our conclusions contradict themselves, we can enter into the courtroom of Scripture, present our case to the highest authority, and the Word of God is the judge that determines what is true and what is not.

God's Word is true. God's truth can be trusted. But our truth is always on trial. Therefore, the only way to discern truth from opinion is to search the Scriptures (John 5:39), for the Word of God is true. It has survived the test of time.

Seeing truth in this way will have an invaluable impact on the way we see and manage our lives. For example, if someone were to ask you if you love God, you would probably say yes. As a matter of fact, you would probably respond with passion and enthusiasm. However, the accuracy of your answer is not determined by you but by Scripture. Scripture reveals the evidence of a heart that loves God, which includes keeping Jesus's commandments, serving the least of these, prioritizing your relationship with God above all others, and operating in financial generosity. You see, self-assessments only reveal where we think we are, but scriptural assessments reveal where we really are. It is only when we honestly assess our lives through the lens of Scripture that we can make real steps toward authentic Christlikeness.

What Is the Value of Truth?

Have you ever heard a person in mourning say, "I just need to know the truth of what happened," even though they cannot change the circumstances of the loss? Perhaps you have sat across the table from an ex who broke your heart. You were sure the relationship was over, but you just needed to know the truth. Your heart needed closure. Your mind longed for details that would be difficult to hear but would put to bed, once and for all, your endless speculation. You needed truth. Our souls find rest in the truth. Even if we cannot change the past, the truth gives us the freedom to move forward.

Truth has one primary purpose: to free us from the prison of falsehood and introduce us to our authentic self. One of my mentors often says, "God only anoints the real you." The only person God will help you become is yourself. Truth protects us from the masquerade of pretention. It liberates us from the temptation to waste time pretending to be someone else. We all, at some point or another, struggle with this tendency. It began with Eve being deceived by the serpent in the garden and resulted in the wrecking of her life. Truth keeps us away from the catastrophe of a ruined life and a damaged reputation.

When we are not people of truth, our energy disappears, our character decays, and our integrity depreciates. Let me put it this way: being someone else is too much work. You end up being a consistent chameleon that has to change colors in different environments and in different contexts. You also rob those around you of the unique blessing that the real you brings.

I'm ecstatic Jesus was true to Himself. I need Him to be. The world needs you to be also. Jesus provides a great example of how. It is profoundly displayed on the night before His crucifixion in the Garden of Gethsemane. This moment brings light to darkness, hope to depravity, and wholeness to the wounded. Notice how truth is being modeled in the following verses:

> He took Peter and the two sons of Zebedee along with him, and he began to be sorrowful and troubled. Then he said to them, "My soul is

21

overwhelmed with sorrow to the point of death. Stay here and keep watch with me."

Going a little farther, he fell with his face to the ground and prayed, "My Father, if it is possible, may this cup be taken from me. Yet not as I will, but as you will."

Then he returned to his disciples and found them sleeping. "Couldn't you men keep watch with me for one hour?" he asked Peter. "Watch and pray so that you will not fall into temptation. The spirit is willing, but the flesh is weak."

—MATTHEW 26:37–41

The Gethsemane narrative captures three ways in which Christ models the kind of truth we should emulate. We should be truthful with ourselves, truthful with God, and truthful with others.

Truthful with ourselves

The first person Jesus had to be truthful to was Himself. In verse 38 Jesus admits, "My soul is overwhelmed with sorrow to the point of death." Prior to admitting this to others, He had to come to terms with it Himself. The pressure of being the Messiah never pushed Him to a place where He was dishonest with Himself. When those words fell from His lips, He was twenty-four hours away from crucifixion. The Garden of Gethsemane literally means "the olive press" because it is located on the slope of the Mount of Olives. Symbolically, the garden represented a pressing time in Jesus's earthly ministry. It was a time of pressure. It was a time of prayer. And when you find yourself in Gethsemane, you can't afford to be dishonest.

Jesus begins His truth-telling with Himself: *I am over-whelmed.* Confession is not just for God. God already knows what we want and need to talk about. But we confess in order to acknowledge our authentic selves. We confess because we recognize there can be no transformation without open and honest communication. Quite simply, you must tell the truth to yourself about yourself. *I'm a liar. I'm a workaholic. I love too hard. I have esteem issues. I mismanage money. I don't like my mother. I don't like my father.* These are truths that set us on the path toward true freedom.

Unfortunately, in religious contexts especially, self-deception is the most dominant form of deception. Some even go so far as to espouse doctrines that encourage the denying of reality under the guise of faith. However, I believe faith doesn't deny reality; it just believes God can change it. But God can't adjust it until we acknowledge it. Therefore, I think you need to call a meeting—and the meeting needs to be with you. There are some things in your life that need to be addressed, and they can't be addressed until you acknowledge them.

Truthful with God

Next, Jesus tells the truth to His heavenly Father. He confesses, "My Father, if it is possible, may this cup be taken from me. Yet not as I will, but as you will" (v. 39). It is only when we are truthful with ourselves that we develop the capacity to move beyond a surface and shallow relationship with God.

And here's the real truth: God can handle the authentic, uninhibited you. When we aren't aware of this, we speak to God about everything but the truth of what we need.

I imagine there are times we are engaging God in prayer and God is wondering, "When are we really going to talk? When are you going to talk about how frustrated, discouraged, and broken you are? When are you going to talk about the esteem issues that inhibit you from acknowledging the things you don't like about yourself? When are we going to talk about what causes you to use the Bible as a window and not a mirror? When can we talk about the truth?"

God doesn't need you to present your "perfect self" to Him. He needs you to present your *real self* to Him. You don't have to communicate in prayer as if you're talking to a distant dignitary. Some people use words in prayer they never use in daily conversation: "O most holy and majestic authority, the One on whom the government rests, I beseech Thee, O blessed and inimitable God of all creation, to bestow upon me the joy of Thy salvation." I am not suggesting that approaching God with that type of language is inappropriate; I am saying that for many, it's not authentic. God wants the authentic you in prayer. God wants you to tell Him exactly what is going on in your heart. Like a mentee confides in a mentor, God wants you to be truthful with Him. If you are afraid, tell Him. If you are hurting, tell Him. Jesus told the truth to His Father, and when He did, He found the strength to move on. When we are truthful with God, we will have the same experience.

Truthful with others

Finally, Jesus tells the truth to others. Remember, this moment is like no other in the history of Jesus's life. He needs His friends to watch with Him, but when He returns from prayer, He finds them sleeping. But notice, Jesus doesn't withhold His feelings of disappointment. Often those who refrain from telling the truth today explode on an innocent bystander tomorrow.

Jesus tells His friends the truth. He asks Peter, "Couldn't you men keep watch with Me for one hour?" In other words, Jesus is displeased with how the disciples handled that moment. He is clearly disappointed, and He vocalizes that truth.

This portrait of truth is a helpful reminder to us. When we are not truthful about what pains us, we end up reacting and responding inappropriately later. Regardless of the pain, we must tell the truth to others.

But let's face it—this is easier said than done. In my experience as a pastor, I have discovered this lesson to be an Achilles' heel for many people. Some people struggle with how to be truthful with others. Thankfully Ephesians 4 provides a curriculum on Christian conduct and communication:

> Then we will no longer be infants, tossed back and forth by the waves, and blown here and there by every wind of teaching and by the cunning and craftiness of people in their deceitful scheming. Instead, *speaking the truth in love*, we will grow to become in every respect the mature body of him who is the head, that is, Christ.
> —EPHESIANS 4:14–15, EMPHASIS ADDED

As Paul gives the church at Ephesus some advice, he suggests that evidence of maturity and a catalyst for maturity is speaking the truth in love. Speaking the truth helps others grow, and it is also an indication of your own growth. When we were children we often spoke the truth without a filter. It seems as if the older we get, the more cautious, coded, and sometimes less truthful we become. However, following in the footsteps of Jesus means maturing spiritually to the point that we speak truth. One way to know someone is no longer an "infant" is when he or she can speak the truth in love.

Remember, Jesus does not walk around saying "I am truth" without revealing that truth. His life is a public billboard testifying to the accuracy of His speech. In the same way, our lives must mimic the message we proclaim. If not, we are a walking contradiction. Paul says we must not only speak truth, but also speak it in love.

What does that mean? Truth cannot be received if it is not packaged in love. Truth without love is like a house without furniture, a car without an engine, a heart without a pulse, a dissertation without comprehensive exams—you need one in order to do the other. Warren W. Wiersbe agrees: "Truth without love is brutality, and love without truth is hypocrisy."[2] Jesus understood this, modeled it, and encouraged us to do the same.

BRIDGING THE GAP

This chasm between truth and love may be one reason Gandhi once said that famous quote: "I like your Christ, but I do not like your Christians." When asked to elaborate on this statement, he said quite directly, "Your Christians are so unlike your Christ," which is the central tension of this book. Scripture consistently uses truth to describe Christ, but does truth come to mind when we think of Christ's followers? Are *we* truthful?

In John 16:13 the Holy Spirit is described as "the Spirit

of truth" (KJV) that guides the believer. But if the truth we preach makes us more bound than free, can we irrefutably claim that His Spirit is always guiding us? Here again lies a tantalizing tension. Jesus epitomizes truthfulness, but the question we must ask and answer is, are Christians as truthful as the Christ they worship?

Without question, Jesus models a truth that never has to raise its voice to be heard. Jesus models a truth that often repeats lessons over and over again until the disciples get it. Jesus's truth was patient, even-tempered, "kind, tenderhearted, forgiving" (Eph. 4:32, KJV), and full of compassion. In the same way, our truth must be spoken in love.

How do we do that? We balance our conversations with sincere affirmation, direct confrontation, and encouragement—in that order. When you need to confront someone, begin the conversation by affirming the relationship. In Matthew 16:17 Jesus calls Simon "blessed." In John 1:42 He changes Simon's name to Peter, which means "rock." In other words, Christ affirms the relationship so that Peter knows, "Above all, I love you. I value you, and I want you to be the best you can be." Later Jesus has to rebuke Peter, but the foundation of love has already been laid.

When you confront others, be clear and concise. Do not simply talk—communicate. Resist the tendency to beat around the bush, and ask God to help you to speak in a language your hearer can understand. You've heard it said many times before: it's not always what you say, but how you say it. It's so true.

Once you confront, then confirm. Encourage your listener. Assure them of your desire to see the relationship grow because of this conversation. Tell the truth, but do so in love. You cannot control their response, but you can surely convey truth God's way.

When we affirm, confront, and encourage, we re-present Christ in a way that honors God. When we speak the truth in love, we reconcile the Christ of the Bible with the Christians who bear His name. Our truth must be communicated in love, or else, in the end, it will be no truth at all.

Chapter 3

JESUS and GRACE

*Grace is the beauty of form under
the influence of freedom.*[1]
—FRIEDRICH SCHILLER

IN HIS BOOK *ReJesus* Alan Hirsch provides a prayer
that was given on the morning of June 7, 1964, at the
Boykin Methodist Church near Raleigh, Mississippi:

> Oh God, our Heavenly Guide, as finite creatures
> of time and as dependent creatures of Thine, we
> acknowledge Thee as our sovereign Lord. Permit
> freedom and the joys thereof to forever reign
> throughout our land. May we...forever have the
> courage of our convictions that we may always
> stand for Thee and our great nation. May the
> sweet cup of brotherly fraternity ever be ours to
> enjoy and build within us that kindred spirit which
> will keep us unified and strong. Engender within
> us that wisdom kindred to honorable decisions
> and the Godly work. By the power of Thy infi-
> nite spirit and the energizing virtue therein, ever
> keep before us our oaths of secrecy and pledges of

> righteousness. Bless us now in this assembly that
> we may honor Thee in all things, we pray in the
> name of Christ, our blessed Savior. Amen.[2]

At first glance, this seems to be an articulate and heart-felt prayer. It very well may be. However, according to Alan Hirsch, this prayer was offered by the grand chaplain of the Ku Klux Klan during a rally the group held in order to declare something of a holy war against the civil rights movement. Hirsch notes that within three months, three civil rights workers were murdered execution-style in Neshoba County, Mississippi, all in the name of a righteous cause. Those who were a part of this Klan movement convinced themselves God had approved, endorsed, and sanctioned their activity. This theology was so embedded in their minds that they even used a burning cross as a statement and symbol of their cause. They obviously had an understanding of Christianity that was inconsistent with the life and the character of its founder, Jesus. And they didn't even know it. They had created a Christianity that was nothing like Christ.

Although activity like this group's represents a very small percentage of those who claim Christianity, the perspective of mainstream Christians can be just as jaded and our language and activity just as vitriolic. We may not literally take someone's life, but through our inclination to be judgmental or self-righteous we take people's esteem, dignity, and hope all in the name of our faith. This is a Christianity without grace.

If the popular acronym is true, then GRACE stands for "God's Riches At Christ's Expense," and Jesus is the fullest embodiment of it. In the last chapter we discussed how

Jesus came into the world full of truth, but remember He also came full of grace (John 1:14). Grace is the operative term for this chapter, and because Jesus embodied it on earth, those who identify as Christ followers should do the same.

The Gospels clearly present Jesus as a man of grace; therefore, a graceless Christianity is a misrepresentation of Jesus. Knowing this cognitively is one thing; living it out is another. Therefore we should turn to Scripture in order to figure out what grace is, where grace shows up in the Bible, and how and when grace is applicable to our current situation.

GRACE CUTS BOTH WAYS

For starters, what is grace? It is much more than the few lines we hurriedly recite over a home-cooked meal. Instead, grace is the unmerited, unearned, and undeserved favor of God. It is when God in His sovereignty, according to the counsel of His own will, decides to extend goodness and benevolence to people who don't deserve it—people like you and me. Grace is so mesmerizing that in 1779, the English poet and preacher John Newton wrote a song about it and called it "Amazing Grace." Its first two stanzas resound:

> Amazing grace, how sweet the sound
> that saved a wretch like me.
> I once was lost but now am found,
> was blind but now I see.
>
> 'Twas grace that taught my heart to fear
> and grace my fears relieved.

How precious did that grace appear
the hour I first believed.[3]

Yes, grace is amazing, and this song captures the essence of grace in beautiful poetic language. At the same time, these lyrics expose a fatal flaw as it pertains to the way most of us view grace. For the most part we see grace as something we receive from God, which is correct but not complete. The other part of grace we seldom grasp is how God calls us to extend that same grace to others just as freely as we have received it from Him.

If we're honest, we all love to be on the receiving end of grace. We don't mind when God gives us what we don't deserve or when He overlooks our heinous offenses. If all we had to do was receive grace, there would be no need to preach about it.

But our true struggle is to give grace to people we feel aren't worthy of it. "They don't deserve it," we think. "They've had too many chances before, and now it's time for them to pay for their sins." We even use prayer as a retaliatory device, as David did when he prayed, "Break their teeth, O God, in their mouth: break out the great teeth of the young lions, O LORD. Let them melt away as waters which run continually... as a snail which melteth, let every one of them pass away" (Ps. 58:6–8, KJV). Why do we do this? Because we want those who have caused us pain to feel pain. We want grace for us but justice for them.

We all struggle with the giving components grace requires. But grace is not an individualized commodity. It isn't something you qualify for if you have good credit or attend fifty worship services per year. Grace is scandalous. It is the Lord dying in our place for sins He never committed in order to save His persecutors and restore humanity by and through His blood, not ours. If you tried to understand it, you'd get a headache. If you tried to explain it, you'd never quite capture it. Grace is the divine character of Jesus Christ, which we both receive and extend.

If we are going to re-present Christ in the world, we must learn to live out grace in its full dualistic nature. We must give just as we receive. One biblical text that provides an amazing example of how to do this is found in John 8:

> But Jesus went to the Mount of Olives.
>
> At dawn he appeared again in the temple courts, where all the people gathered around him, and he sat down to teach them. The teachers of the law and the Pharisees brought in a woman caught in adultery. They made her stand before the group and said to Jesus, "Teacher, this woman was caught in the act of adultery. In the Law Moses commanded us to stone such women. Now what do you say?" They were using this question as a trap, in order to have a basis for accusing him.
>
> But Jesus bent down and started to write on the ground with his finger. When they kept on questioning him, he straightened up and said to them, "Let any one of you who is without sin be the first to throw a stone at her." Again he stooped down and wrote on the ground.
>
> At this, those who heard began to go away one at a time, the older ones first, until only Jesus was left, with the woman still standing there. Jesus

straightened up and asked her, "Woman, where are they? Has no one condemned you?"

"No one, sir," she said.

"Then neither do I condemn you," Jesus declared. "Go now and leave your life of sin."

—John 8:1–11

The Backstory

In this passage an unnamed woman is about to be stoned for committing adultery. Jesus is in the temple teaching a crowd of people when all of a sudden an onslaught of Jewish leaders interrupt Him. In their arms is a helpless woman. She's probably being brought to the temple by force and placed in front of a crowd without her consent, only for the leaders to demand of Jesus, "Stone her according to the law!"

But Jesus does not respond. He doesn't respond because He knows these men have impure motives. The text reveals, "They were using this question as a trap, in order to have a basis for accusing Jesus" (v. 6). You see, some trick questions are actually trap questions, and as Christ followers we must discern the difference. The reality was, this situation wasn't about the woman; it was about using her bad day to condemn Christ interminably. It was a catch-22, because if Jesus went against the law, they could accuse Him of blasphemy. But if He called for them to administer the law, they could accuse Him before the Romans. Jews were not allowed to execute someone; only Romans could (John 18:31). Jesus knew their intentions, so He said nothing.

Another reason we can see an ulterior motive here is because the religious leaders were not applying the law accurately. The law plainly states that both the man and woman must be put to death in instances of adultery (Lev. 20:10). Here, they had only the woman, so they were trying to apply Scripture with a selective and subjective twist. They said she was caught in the act. But where was the man? They had not applied the law correctly. So Jesus kneels down and starts doodling in the dust. He is writing in the sand. They demand a response, but Jesus does not budge or oblige.

When Jesus is ready, He stands up and says these memorable words: "Let any one of you who is without sin be the first to throw a stone at her" (John 8:7). Jesus was speaking their language because He knew they knew what Deuteronomy 17:7 said: "The hands of the witnesses must be the first in putting that person to death, and then the hands of all the people." In other words, the witnesses had to throw the stone first. When Jesus challenges them to rethink their accusation by looking within the arsenals of their own sinfulness, they stop in their tracks. He then kneels back down and starts to write again—and one by one, the accusers leave.

Theologians debate what Jesus wrote on the ground that day, but no one truly knows except Jesus, the religious leaders, and the woman who was at the mercy of a grace-filled Christ. It could be that Jesus was writing sins in the sand, and when He got to theirs, they decided to make their exit. It could be Jesus was writing the name of the man who committed the act with her or the names of each accuser standing in front of Him. Regardless of what He wrote, when Jesus stood back up, there was no one around to stone the woman.

So Jesus asks the woman, "Who is here to condemn

you?" She replies, "No one." He then responds, "Neither do I, go and sin no more." Most of us see this as a happily-ever-after story. But in order to see this text through the lens of grace, we must understand the significance of Jesus's final statement to this woman.

Deuteronomy 19:15 tells us you cannot convict anyone of a crime on the testimony of only one witness. Jesus's doodling in the dust ran the witnesses away. This is an amazing example of what grace does. Grace uses the same word others used to keep you bound in order to set you free. Grace takes the same book that says "Don't touch it" to help you recover after you do touch it. The same book that convicts us can also comfort us. The same book that makes us frown is the very book that makes us smile. The same Bible that says, "The wages of sin is death" (Rom. 6:23), also tells us, "If we confess our sins, [God] is faithful and just to forgive us our sins, and to cleanse us from all unrighteousness" (1 John 1:9, KJV). That is the grace of God at work. It never compromises the law, but it locates the loopholes to get us out of the stronghold of legalism. If the law had its way, each of us would be serving a life sentence. But Jesus came into the world full of grace to take our place, dismiss our case, and grant us a life we never deserved.

Now, I can hear many of you silently suggesting my presentation of grace here is absent of accountability. You may be thinking it ignores the moral standard of Scripture and asserts that anything goes. However, I am saying the exact opposite. Grace doesn't lower God's standard; it is simply a better motivator for reaching it. As a matter of fact, grace helps us reach the standard. Grace is multifaceted. The apostle Peter says in 1 Peter 4:10 that

God's grace is manifold. In other words, it has various forms. Grace doesn't just excuse us; it also enables us. It assists us in living a life consistent with the virtues, values, and vantage points of Jesus.

These conclusions are refreshing to know as recipients of grace. But remember we are called to distribute that grace as well. The way Jesus responds to this woman is the way we are to respond to others.

For this reason, I want to consider three questions: Who does this woman represent in our present day? What modern stones might be thrown at people like her? And what can we learn from Jesus's response in order to be better carriers of grace?

What Jesus Teaches Us

The woman in John 8 could be any one of us reading this book today. She represents anyone whose private failure has become public knowledge. She could be the latest politician involved in a scandal or the pastor whose name shows up in the newspaper. She could be a coworker or a classmate caught between the fierce winds of a rumor mill or the innocent bystander who just so happened to be in the wrong place at the wrong time.

The stones we use to hurt her could be tweets or Facebook posts or any number of technological weapons intended to attack and destroy. You've seen their power of destruction, I'm sure. Stones are accusatory conversations that kill a person's reputation or hearsay allegations that result in the fracturing of one's family. When the church does this, when people participate in this, and when we choose this, we are just like the Pharisees in this story.

The one thing the Pharisees did right in this text was walk away. Sometimes there are situations that have nothing to do with us, and instead of gossiping about something we can't confirm or deny, we should just walk away and pray. Situations that don't affect you or your family personally should be situations from which you simply walk away.

One of my favorite New Testament scriptures corroborates the importance of this point. In 1 Thessalonians 4:11, Paul writes to the church and says, "Make it your ambition to lead a quiet life: you should mind your own business and work with your own hands, just as we told you." It's as simple as that. Everything does not require our surveillance or commentary. God has not called us to be the moral police. We are called to live out our faith, not legislate it. Sometimes we need to mind our business and handle our own work. When people wander into other people's personal lives, it usually ends in trouble.

Now this doesn't mean we should ignore the needs of others. For example, if you are in relationship with someone, you can't just look away. In some instances we are absolutely under a moral and biblical obligation to help those in need. But the greater lesson is to recognize we aren't called to be the church police. Our job is not to keep everyone else's life under our surveillance. So prayerfully consider and think through what God is calling you to do in each situation. And if by chance you decide to help someone who has fallen short of God's glory, be sure to bathe your help in grace. Jesus was the best example of this. He knew when to speak and He knew when to be silent. But ultimately, in every moment, He showed grace.

Jesus's example not only reveals that we should show grace but how we can do so. In this same scriptural passage, Jesus models exactly what it looks like to walk this fine line. He reveals three specific ways He manages this situation with grace. First, He shows compassion for the person without condoning the activity. Second, He communicates with the woman without compromising His position. Finally, He challenges her to a higher level of living without condemning her. Through Jesus's example, we are called and challenged to do likewise.

Step #1: Compassion without condoning

Let's be clear about something. This woman was guilty, and she was wrong. Her sin was not pretty; it was heinous. However, we may have a lot more in common with her than we think.

You may be asking, "How can I relate to this woman in the text?" And my answer is, everybody has had a bad day. Good people not only have bad days; we also have bad seasons. So the only difference between this woman and us is that no one wrote a book about our bad day. No one filed a report listing our ten most shameful sins and published it in the canon of Scripture for the entire world to know and scrutinize. We may not have all committed the sin of adultery to natural spouses. However, we are all a part of the bride of Christ, and we have all committed acts of unfaithfulness to our groom, Jesus.

God frequently used the analogy of adultery to describe Israel's unfaithfulness to Him in the Old Testament. The entire Book of Hosea, for example, charts a dark and melancholic era of Israel's history because the people had turned away from God in order to serve the calves of Jeroboam and Baal, a Canaanite god. As God's prophet, Hosea was directed by God to marry a promiscuous woman of ill repute in order to symbolically represent the covenantal relationship between God and Israel. Gomer was a prostitute and Israel was, in like manner, a harlot. When Gomer married Hosea, she continued to be promiscuous outside of her covenant, but Hosea loved her anyway. Although Hosea removed Gomer from the streets, the streets did not leave her. She was married but continued to go back to the red light district for a tentative fling. Still, Hosea would find her, rescue her, provide for her, love her, and cherish her. Time after time he would display unconditional love toward her, but in a matter of days, she would run back to her familiar red lights.

The devotion Hosea displayed toward Gomer mirrors the way God devotes Himself to us. God was using Hosea's life as a portrait for how He dealt with Israel even when they ran off. All of us at one time or another have been unfaithful to God. All of us have compromised our Christian witness in some way. And it is this awareness of our struggles that should provoke us to have compassion for others without condoning their sin. The word *compassion* refers to a sense of empathy for the plight of others. Jesus, who was sinless, demonstrated compassion for this woman. If it is possible for the One who is sinless to show compassion for those who have fallen, why can't we?

The religious leaders in this woman's story were void of compassion. However, Jesus challenges them by saying, "He who is without sin, let him cast the first stone" (John 8:7). Notice He did not say, "He who is without this *particular* sin, cast the stone." Why? Because Jesus wanted the Pharisees to know that sin is sin. There is no caste system of sins. Some Christians live with that mind-set, you know. They think, "I've done this, but at least I haven't done that." This kind of thinking is inconsistent with Scripture. As a matter of fact, Jesus deals with this kind of attitude in Luke 18:

> The Pharisee stood by himself and prayed: "God, I thank you that I am not like other people—robbers, evildoers, adulterers—or even like this tax collector. I fast twice a week and give a tenth of all I get."
>
> But the tax collector stood at a distance. He would not even look up to heaven, but beat his breast and said, "God, have mercy on me, a sinner."
>
> I tell you that this man, rather than the other, went home justified before God. For all those who exalt themselves will be humbled, and those who humble themselves will be exalted.
>
> —LUKE 18:11–14

We all from time to time have the "I haven't done that and I'm not like them" syndrome. When we're not aware of it, we can become filled with pride instead of compassion. Showing compassion doesn't mean we condone the activity the person is doing, but it does mean we know what it's like to be Gomer. Therefore, we have an obligation to demonstrate the same type of grace to others that God has given to us. We have received it freely, and we must give it freely.

This kind of grace solidifies our love for God. When we are unfaithful, He remains faithful. When we run away,

He comes to where we are. When we mess up, He writes on the ground so that our accusers have no choice but to walk away.

Step #2: Communicate without compromising

Not only did Jesus show compassion for the woman without condoning her activity, but He also communicated with her without compromising His position. The silent treatment may work on students but not sinners. You can't win people you won't talk to. Often when people's secret sins are exposed, the first thing they do is run away. The one who is guilty looks for a place to hide, and his friends disappear. We do this because we are uncomfortable being affiliated with drama and scandal. We don't want to be associated with duplicitous behavior.

But Jesus doesn't respond the way most of us would have responded. Instead of running away from this woman, He speaks directly to her. He communicates compassion without compromising His position. He engages this woman without lowering His standards.

All throughout Jesus's earthly ministry we find Him conversing with controversial figures. In John 4, for instance, He is having a conversation at the well with a woman from Samaria. During that time Jews didn't talk to Samaritans and men didn't talk to women in public. So it makes sense why verse 27 says, "His disciples returned and were surprised to find him talking with a woman. But not one asked, 'What do you want?' or 'Why are you talking with her?'"

With each conversation He had, Jesus was changing the face of grace. He understood what some of us are still struggling to accept—that is, people cannot receive the help they need unless someone talks to them first. If no one speaks, how will they get better? How can they hear without a preacher? How can they repent if no dialogue occurs? How would the woman with the issue of blood receive healing if no one dared to get close enough to tell her Jesus was in town?

Grace is communication without compromise. Our goal is always restoration, not condemnation. Galatians 6:1 confirms this when Paul tells the churches, "If someone is caught in a sin, you who live by the Spirit should restore that person gently. But watch yourselves, or you also may be tempted." Another translation says, "If a man is overtaken in a fault, ye which are spiritual, restore such an one" (KJV).

The first criterion is the challenge. The word *spiritual* does not mean Spirit-filled; rather, Paul is asking if they are Spirit-*led*. When we are led by the Spirit, restoration is our destination. There simply cannot be restoration in the absence of communication. Even though "sinners"—and I put that in quotes because aren't we all sinners?—have been pushed to the margins of society, someone has to engage them. Even though they have lost their way in the faith, someone has to speak to their hearts in a Christlike manner. Somebody has to remind them, "Where sin increased, grace increased all the more" (Rom. 5:20).

And guess what? You are the someone God is looking for! You are the one God wants to use in the midst of a dying world. God is relying on your words to say, "Listen, I know you messed up, and I know you are suffering, but God is your great redeemer. See how God redeemed David? In the same way, He can redeem you!" If we are going to re-present Christ, then we cannot abandon people when they need Him the most. Jesus didn't abandon us, so who are we to abandon others?

Step #3: Challenge without condemning

The conversation with the adulterous woman ends with a challenge. Jesus makes it very clear we are not to condemn sinners, but He also clarifies the difference between condemnation and challenge. In this text Jesus challenges the woman to change her lifestyle. His method is a model for how we are to lovingly confront people in similar situations.

Jesus says to her, "Go and sin no more" (John 8:11, NKJV). That's all He says. He doesn't add, "Go and sin no more, you nasty scoundrel." He doesn't say, "Even though God forgives, you know you were wrong for what you did, and you need to repent." He says nothing of the sort. His words are empty of judgment and full of compassion. He simply tells her what she needs to do next.

Here's what we are being asked to learn from this: When speaking to people who have been caught in sin, remove all judgmental, condescending, and infantilizing language. Love covers a multitude of sins. Only the love of God will draw us back to the Father, so refrain from stating the obvious. Refrain from painful prose. This woman already knew she was wrong. She knew she had sinned before God. We don't need to add insult to injury. We are not prophetic policemen and policewomen. Instead, model the attributes of Romans 2:4: reflect the richness of God's kindness, forbearance, and patience, for that is the only way others will be led into repentance.

When Jesus dispels the woman's accusers, forgives her

sins, and challenges her to change, He personifies His heavenly mission on earth. Remember where it started? God so loved the world that He gave His only begotten son so that those who believe in Him would not perish, but have everlasting life. As we already learned, the next verse gives the proverbial home run: God did not send His Son into the world to condemn the world, but to save the world through Him. When you connect John 3:16–17 to this text in John 8, it is clear Jesus showed this woman a preview of salvation by grace through faith.

The gift of grace, just like salvation, is not earned because of us; it is granted in spite of us. It is a gift from God, not by works, so that no one can boast (Eph. 2:9). We must never forget the gift of grace given to us by and in Jesus Christ. We must never forget the one chapter in our lives that reveals the truth of our similarity to this woman who was caught in an act of sinfulness. We must never forget that all people may fall but we are to be the ones who pick them up, not finish them off. Jesus did it for us. Let's do it for others.

Chapter 4

JESUS and WISDOM

*Wisdom is the right use of knowledge. To know
is not to be wise. Many men know a great deal,
and are all the greater fools for it. There is no
fool so great a fool as a knowing fool. But to
know how to use knowledge is to have wisdom.*[1]
—CHARLES SPURGEON

O NE COLD WINTER night an old woman received
a knock at her door. She opened it, and to her
surprise, found three tall wizard-looking men
standing on her porch. The first man motioned toward
her and said, "My name is Wealth. His name is Wellbeing, and that guy over there...his name is Wisdom."

She smiled at these strangers and said, "Nice to meet
you. It sure is cold out there. Would you all like to come
inside for a moment?"

Wealth spoke up and said, "That's the problem. You
can only invite one of us into your home. But take your
time and choose carefully. The two men whom you don't
choose will have to stay behind."

The woman hadn't expected such a challenge but was

excited about the proposition. So she thought long and hard about her options. She could surely use a few more dollars, but wealth without wellbeing would not buy her happiness—and she needed to be happy even if she was homeless. And then there was wisdom, which seemed like a good idea, but the woman didn't know how wisdom could help meet her immediate needs. Confused by her options and shivering from the cold, she quickly played eeny, meeny, miny, moe, and stopped on Wisdom.

"Welp. There you have it: Wisdom. Come on in!" She stepped aside to welcome her new friend, and all three men entered the door.

Shocked, the woman whispered, "But I thought you said only one could come in."

Wisdom replied, "Well, that was the other stipulation you didn't know about. If you had chosen Wealth or Wellbeing, the other two of us would've had to stay behind. But when you chose me, you got all three."

Imagine that for a nice surprise at the door—wealth, wellbeing, and wisdom, all asking for permission to enter your home! If you were that woman, which would you have chosen? You may not realize it, but one of these three is bargaining for your time right now. One of these three is pulling on your energy, shopping for your attention, and either refueling you or removing something from you.

Everything you do will either yield wealth, wellbeing, wisdom, or the lack thereof. But is wisdom as attractive to you as those other options? King Solomon would say yes, and I'm sure Jesus would say the same. In fact, Jesus did not just choose wisdom, He *embodied* it. So He never had to worry about wealth, wellness, health, wholeness, or anything in between.

I think part of the problem with contemporary Christianity is that most of us still believe it is something we do, not necessarily something we are. When we ask ourselves "How can I become a better Christian?" we immediately run toward answers that tend to focus on morality and behavior. We think about habits we need to break and relationships we need to do away with.

I wonder if you are aware of how important it is to not simply behave like a Christian, but also to think like one, to decide like one, and to plan like one. It is our thinking that determines our behavior, not the other way around. Everything we end up doing flows from the riverbed of what we know and how we put what we know into practice. It matters how we receive information, how we translate that information, and how we capitalize on our previous experiences. This in a nutshell is the virtue of wisdom. When we finally understand the importance of wisdom, we will move from the tentative state of *doing* Christianity to the permanent state of *being* a Christian.

In previous chapters we discussed different ways we are meant to behave as Christians—demonstrating love, speaking truth, and offering grace. If we are going to re-present Christ, we must learn how to do all these things. But this chapter steps beyond our comfort zone of Christian morality to discuss ways of being and thinking. We are moving from conduct to character here because it is our thinking that controls our doing—and when Christians begin to see godliness as more than moral living, we will become even greater Christian witnesses. If we are going to be Christ's ambassadors in culture and re-present Him to the world around us, then we must passionately pursue and prioritize wisdom, just like He did.

GOT WISDOM?

Wisdom is so essential to a godly life that God devoted an entire section of the Bible to it, called wisdom literature. Job, Psalms, Proverbs, Ecclesiastes, and Song of Songs are all books that comprise this genre in Scripture. As such, they impart experience, knowledge, and practical principles into the hearts and minds of every reader who is willing to learn from human snapshots. Most certainly, if we were to spend more time acquiring wisdom, we would save ourselves from the tragedy of repeating someone else's life lesson.

In Job we learn the importance of worship in spite of the losses. Job teaches believers how to handle life's unexpected blows and gives us permission to be human and holy. In Psalms we encounter ballads, laments, and prayers that confront sorrow, abandonment, loss, and forgiveness. If we learn from the writers in Psalms, we have a guide to keep us from the snares of depression, guilt, and isolation. Both Ecclesiastes and Proverbs deliver slices of wisdom for practical living. When we read those books, we learn how to relate to one another and how to value God over material possessions. Finally, Song of Songs is the wisdom text that invites us to enjoy the harmony that love brings. It is the dance between two lovers who value reciprocity, passion, and joy—three words that many of us continue to struggle with in private and public relationships. Thus each book has its own focus and theme, but together these wise words have been written to prevent us from enduring a Christian life without practical guideposts to live by.

We are all aware that life can throw us curveballs. We can end up facing unpredictable and often unavoidable circumstances. Because life will give us our own set of headaches from time to time, we should avoid creating any extra ones for ourselves. Living with a lack of wisdom is an invitation for unnecessary inconveniences. It is the equivalent of sending trouble an e-vite to your home and hoping it doesn't RSVP. If we're honest with ourselves, some challenging seasons in our lives weren't an attack of the enemy but rather the result of a wisdom deficiency.

One example I frequently witness is in the relationship arena. The demographic I serve at this point in my ministry is one that is heavily populated with young adults. Therefore, I frequently encounter crises and questions surrounding dating. Some of the crises are probably unavoidable. But others could have been avoided by simply using wisdom. For example, Paul tells the believers at Corinth not to be unequally yoked with unbelievers (2 Cor. 6:14). He used a metaphor that has roots in Deuteronomy 22:10, where Israel is commanded not to yoke an ox and donkey together. Oxen and donkeys have two completely different natures. It will be extremely difficult to get them to work productively if they are yoked together, because donkeys have historically been noncompliant. This aspect of a donkey's personality can represent our unregenerate nature, which can be stubborn and noncompliant also. Paul was warning the regenerate of the danger of "yoking up" with the unregenerate, because even if it didn't seem immoral, it was definitely unwise.

Although Paul is not speaking specifically about dating and marital relationships in this passage, it surely applies to those relationships. Therefore, to attempt to build a future with someone whose value system is different than yours, whose allegiance to Jesus is not like yours, and whose commitment to growth isn't consistent with yours, is an invite for a headache. Many who are reading this book can look back to some headaches and heartaches that could have been avoided if they had used wisdom.

Another example is in the financial arena. The Scriptures speak of the importance of stewardship, which includes budgeting, living within our means, debt reduction, and saving. Many of us have experienced seasons of financial pressure and stress because we overextended ourselves and failed to budget properly and live with financial margin. This may not be immoral, but it is unwise and it creates unnecessary chaos in our lives. I am not saying that all financial strain and stress is a result of something we did or didn't do. I am saying that there are seasons when we experience things like this unnecessarily because of the absence of wisdom. We need wisdom.

Wisdom is key to a life that is salt and light. The life the Scriptures reveal is unattainable independent of wisdom. Your gifts may empower others to become great, but wisdom will help *you* to become great. Wisdom will speak to you and say "Rest" even when others are begging you to show up. Wisdom will teach you how to manage the pressure of family, work, school, and love.

Wisdom saves you from the exhaustion of life's never-ending to-do lists. If you grasp it now, you will save yourself the trauma of a life lived on repeat, cycling through the same old mistakes again and again.

It's More Than Morality

Jesus is the wisest person who has ever walked the face of the earth. That's right—He isn't just spiritual, He's smart. Wisdom is interwoven into the fabric of His character. And remember, when we see Jesus, we see God the Father, because "anyone who has seen [Christ] has seen the Father" (John 14:9). Therefore, when we see Jesus, we learn how the Father thinks, responds, and reacts, and also how He desires us to do the same for the purpose of godly living.

I alluded to this earlier, but I must repeat it for clarification: godliness is often myopically minimized to mean morality. Some Christian contexts look for and demand that Christians "live right." However, Jesus's life teaches us that living right is not just about moral excellence; it also includes wise decision making. Godliness is always undergirded by wisdom, not postured in competition against it. It includes morality but is more than morality. It is more than "living right." It is also living wisely.

Therefore, growing in godliness means growing in wisdom—just as Jesus did. Luke says, "And Jesus grew in wisdom and stature, and in favor with God and man" (Luke 2:52). The sequence of events matters here. He first grew in wisdom and in stature. His inner man was developed in wisdom, which provoked an outer manifestation of favor with God and man.

Did you know that when you grow in wisdom, you

automatically grow in favor as well? And what is favor? It's when God providentially orchestrates preferential treatment toward you that you can't earn. It's when someone has to be selected for an opportunity and out of all who could have been picked, you were selected. It is when the scholarship, the internship, the promotion, the invite, the access just so happens to land in your lap. This truth is present in all of Scripture, but an amazing example is found in John 5. Jesus visits a place called Bethesda that was populated with those who were sick and infirm. Jesus just so happens to walk over to a man who had been afflicted with an undisclosed infirmity for thirty-eight years and asks him if he wants to be made whole. Out of all the people in the place who probably wanted healing, this one man received it. However, it was this man's wisdom that put him in the position to receive the miracle. Each year he consistently pressed his way to Bethesda and lay by the pool. He didn't earn the favor, but he positioned himself to receive it. We can't earn favor, but wisdom puts us in position to receive. When we embrace wisdom it positions us for favor.

Favor is fragile, though—it must be handled with hands controlled by a heart of wisdom. A fool will fumble favor, but a wise man or woman will maintain it. Jesus is a wise man, and He admonishes us to also be people of wisdom: "Be ye therefore wise as serpents, and harmless as doves" (Matt. 10:16, KJV).

HEARING AND DOING

In Matthew 7, Jesus provides some guidance on how to practically pursue growth in this virtue called wisdom. Read these verses as if you are reading them for the first time. Pay attention to the differences between a wise builder and a foolish one:

> "Therefore everyone who hears these words of mine and puts them into practice is like a wise man who built his house on the rock. The rain came down, the streams rose, and the winds blew and beat against that house; yet it did not fall, because it had its foundation on the rock. But everyone who hears these words of mine and does not put them into practice is like a foolish man who built his house on sand. The rain came down, the streams rose, and the winds blew and beat against that house, and it fell with a great crash."
>
> When Jesus had finished saying these things, the crowds were amazed at his teaching, because he taught as one who had authority, and not as their teachers of the law.
>
> —MATTHEW 7:24–29

The full chapter of Matthew 7 is all about dichotomies. As the chapter opens, we find Jesus crafting a conversational web of sorts. He lays out key differences between a true prophet and a false prophet, a true disciple versus a false disciple, and the difference between seeking God and judging others. In an earlier portion of the chapter He talks about two roads—a narrow one and wide one—and then two trees that bear good and bad fruit. Now in verse 24 He talks about two houses.

If you focus on the images of all these metaphors, you will totally miss the point. Jesus is less concerned with the kind of pavement being used or the actual cost of the house being built. His concern has all to do with the internal and foundational parts of these images.

When speaking of wisdom, Jesus begins, "Whoever hears these words and puts them into practice is wise." Let's think about that for a moment. In one short sentence, Jesus encapsulates the wisdom question. He says, "This is how it happens." Simultaneously He presents two major challenges to His hearers. In order to acquire wisdom, Jesus first contends we must be exceptional hearers. He doesn't say, "Read more, work harder, or become rich." He simply says, "Hear, and you shall be wise."

Second, we must put what we hear into practice. Showing up to the lecture doesn't make a student smart. It is when the student listens to the professor, translates the information into application, and then uses what he has heard in order to change what he has done that he truly learns and demonstrates that learning. This is what makes us wise builders too—hearing and doing.

But in order to hear what needs to be heard, we must be in a position to receive it. Allow me the opportunity to explain what I mean.

CAN YOU HEAR?

Think about your teenage child or your grad school friend who walks into a room with headphones in her ears and music blasting. If you try to speak, even if you scream her name, she won't be able to hear you because the music is blocking her from doing so. The same is true for many of us. Jesus is trying to speak words of wisdom into our lives through various means—through pastors, family members, billboards we drive past on our way to work, people we overlook before we arrive to our destination—but our hearing can be impaired if we are too busy to hear Him.

In order to hear God, we must be in the right place at the right time with the right posture. Position matters. If the devil cannot make you bad, he will make you busy. If he can't make you unmotivated, he will waste your time by having you do things you don't really need to do. If he can't steal your zeal, he will rip away your focus. Why? So we don't make listening to God a priority.

Jesus addressed this issue with two sisters named Mary and Martha:

> As Jesus and his disciples were on their way, he came to a village where a woman named Martha opened her home to him. She had a sister called Mary, who sat at the Lord's feet listening to what he said. But Martha was distracted by all the preparations that had to be made. She came to him and asked, "Lord, don't you care that my sister has left me to do the work by myself? Tell her to help me!"
>
> "Martha, Martha," the Lord answered, "you are worried and upset about many things, but few things are needed—or indeed only one. Mary has chosen what is better, and it will not be taken away from her."
>
> —LUKE 10:38–42

Martha was distracted by all of the preparation, but Mary had positioned herself at Jesus's feet to hear and receive His instruction. Which sister do you think exemplified wisdom? Some would say Martha because she knew she had to prepare for Jesus, but Jesus says, "Mary has chosen what is better." How does this apply to us?

You might try to convince yourself you can hear Jesus while getting the kids ready for school, preparing breakfast, and getting dressed for work all at the same time, but I want you to know it is absolutely impossible to do so. Wisdom is not just caught; it is also taught. To receive it, you must give God your attention, like Mary did.

Isn't it funny how we become so busy doing things to secure material things that can be taken away but miss out on the spiritual things that can't be taken away? For example, we might work overtime for a car, house, or degree on the wall, but all those things are revocable. The better thing would be to focus on that which is in your heart and in your head, because wisdom is a gift that can never be lost. As long as you have the wisdom to make solid decisions, you can purchase another house, own another car, and obtain another degree.

The diabolical trick is aimed toward getting you to expend your energy on things that don't accumulate spiritual interest in your life. If you decide to stay home from church because you feel you're just too busy to go, for example, that may seem inconsequential on the surface. But if going to church is the most consistent means you have for receiving godly wisdom and instruction so you can make better decisions, the foolish thing would be to skip it. God provides ample opportunities for us to receive wisdom and enhance our lives through prayer, studying the Word, being taught the Word, and godly relationships, but if we are so hurried and busy like Martha, we will miss our greatest blessing on the way to our biggest distraction.

Not only is it important to be in the right place at the right time—remember, Mary and Martha were in the same house with Jesus, but only one of them was listening—we must also be in the right mental space. Wisdom is the recognition that "I don't have to be everywhere to make my presence known." There are some events that require your absence and others that require your presence. There are some family functions you cannot afford to miss and others for which a nice card and flowers serve as a sufficient and thoughtful exchange of love. Jesus did not show up at every wedding or heal in every town. His disciples were charged to go to some places to do ministry while being prohibited from going to other places. How do we know which to do when? We sit at the feet of Jesus not just to hear His words but also to do them. This is wisdom in action.

LISTEN FOR GOD'S VOICE

Notice what Jesus says about wise building—that the wise man hears His sayings. The wise man doesn't hear *every* saying. He doesn't equate the words of Christ with the words of a best-selling author or life coach. Instead, he or she concentrates on what God says and prioritizes God's Word over the cacophony of human opinion.

It's extremely important to filter the words of faith from the words of popular voices. Sometimes our foolish actions come directly from our inability to elevate God's voice over and above our own. I mean, let's be honest. There are times when our thoughts and opinions have caused us to get into a load of trouble. We didn't know how to decipher what God was saying from what we wanted Him to say, and when we finally made a decision, we opted for our wants instead of His will. This is not wisdom, friends; this is arrogance. Any time we assume we know more than God or imagine we don't need to sit at Jesus's feet to receive instruction from God or someone being used by God, we are operating in arrogance. But wisdom and arrogance cannot coexist in the same mental house. This is why Scripture teaches us not to be wise in our own eyes. Arrogance is an inhibitor to wisdom. Wisdom dispels all arrogance. In order to think like Jesus and make wise decisions like Jesus, we must accept the fact that—I'm about to say something really deep!—*God is smarter than us, and we should act like it.* Just as Jesus did.

In Mark 13:32, when speaking of the Father's return, Jesus said, "But about that day or hour no one knows, not even the angels in heaven, nor the Son, but only the Father." Let me remind you, readers: Jesus is God. He and the Father are one. Yet Jesus did not pretend to know more than the Father had revealed to Him. If this was the case for Christ, then who are we in comparison? As mere mortals, we have no right to assume we know anything more than what the Father has revealed to us. When we embrace wisdom, we discard arrogance. When we encounter Christ, we realize how insignificant our intelligence is in comparison to an all-knowing God. Then and only then will we be in the right position to hear God and do what He says.

How Do You Do?

The Book of James gives us great insight into what "doing the Word" looks like. Listen to what James says:

> Who is wise and understanding among you? Let them show it by their good life, by deeds done in

the humility that comes from wisdom. But if you harbor bitter envy and selfish ambition in your hearts, do not boast about it or deny the truth. Such "wisdom" does not come down from heaven but is earthly, unspiritual, demonic. For where you have envy and selfish ambition, there you find disorder and every evil practice.

But the wisdom that comes from heaven is first of all pure; then peace-loving, considerate, submissive, full of mercy and good fruit, impartial and sincere.

—JAMES 3:13–17

We would do well to commit these verses to memory, for in them we receive a menu of instructions for wise living!

Think about your close relationships. How many friends do you have who are pure, peaceful, loving, considerate, full of mercy, and sincere? Now consider the other side of the coin. How many loved ones harbor bitterness, selfish ambition, or envy in their hearts? Even more important than those questions is this one: Where do *you* fall in line with these characteristics?

If wisdom is honest and pure, then we must be honest enough to examine our shortcomings. A great many of us, I imagine, struggle with being peaceful, loving, and considerate 100 percent of the time. Perhaps this is why James 1:22 charges us to not merely "listen to the Word, and so deceive [ourselves]" but to "do what it says." These are sharp words to hear, but they're true and exact.

Listening is deceptive. Hearing a motivational speech will only incite potential within you, not production. You may think things will change if you listen without acting, but they won't. Psalm 1:1–3 says:

> Blessed is the one who does not walk in step with the wicked or stand in the way that sinners take or sit in the company of mockers, but whose delight is in the law of the Lord, and who meditates on his law day and night. That person is like a tree planted by streams of water, which yields its fruit in season and whose leaf does not wither— whatever they do prospers.

Whatever a wise person *does* will prosper—not what he or she *intends* on doing. Now, let's combine these wise words with the Matthew 7 text. The wise man does not walk with or consult unwise counsel. He does not stand in the way of sin or sit with those whose purpose is only to distract him. Wise people do not waste time doing nothing. Instead, they listen to the words of Christ and follow it up with action.

When a wise man builds his house, which is representative of his life, nothing can destroy it. Its foundation is sure and secure. So whether your life includes relationship issues, business matters, or financial decisions, everything you do must be secured on the rock, which is the person of Christ and His unchanging truth. Certainly the rains will come and the floods will rise. Of course the winds will blow and try to beat against your house. These are all natural elements of life, regardless of your foundation. They serve as metaphors of unavoidable occurrences in your life. Being wise does not exempt you from such life-altering experiences; it just keeps your house from sinking. All of us will encounter heartbreak, sickness, or death, but the foundation that wisdom secures will change how these elements affect your core.

If your house is built on sand, then you are unstable and tentative. Your mind will change like the weather, and depending on today's fad, you will alter your convictions to follow your own personal logic at that particular time. These are not dependable characteristics. When natural disasters hit, depending on the day, you may sink or swim. But wisdom promises a house that will always remain intact. Yes, you may endure difficult times, but you will not sink. Your relationship will stand, your business will stand, and your life will stand—all because you have been built on the rock, and that rock is Jesus.

Chapter 5

JESUS and the S-WORD

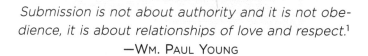

Submission is not about authority and it is not obedience, it is about relationships of love and respect.[1]
—Wm. Paul Young

OVER THE LAST few years, the world has become fascinated with and obsessed by the insatiable need to live a purposeful life. *Purpose, purpose, purpose*—it's all we hear nowadays! Many desire to move past working simply to accumulate wealth or financial gain. We want to work where we are most fulfilled. We want to live deliberately and intentionally. We want our lives to mean something, our investments to matter, and our relationships to thrive.

The desire to live purposefully comes directly from this question: *What am I here for?* And at base level there is nothing wrong with asking it. It is absolutely OK to want to live by purpose and on purpose. Where the problem comes in, I think, is when we try to live our purpose outside of the context of God's plan. Asking the question is not enough. Merely obtaining an awareness of one's purpose is only the first step toward actually accomplishing it.

Jesus unequivocally understood His purpose. What we know about Him is not only recorded in the Scriptures, but it also comes directly from His own lips. It is Jesus who said, "Before Abraham was, I am" (John 8:58, KJV). It is Jesus who declared in the synagogue, "The Spirit of the Lord is upon me, because he hath anointed me to preach the gospel to the poor; he hath sent me to heal the brokenhearted, to preach deliverance to the captives, and recovering of sight to the blind, to set at liberty them that are bruised" (Luke 4:18, KJV). When Jesus finished quoting this text—which would have been a very familiar passage to His hearers—He closed the book, looked at His audience, and said, "Today *this* scripture is fulfilled in your hearing" (Luke 4:21, emphasis added). In other words, "I am the one about whom Isaiah was speaking." Jesus never had an identity crisis. He knew what He was purposed to do in the earth. But knowing His purpose did not automatically mean He accomplished it.

You have a purpose as well. Your presence on the planet is not an accident. God is sovereign. Your life has meaning and your life has purpose, and you have always been in God's plans. However, knowing that is not enough. As a matter of fact, even having some sense of what your purpose is isn't enough. There is a difference between knowing it and fulfilling it.

Therefore, I believe the questions we should attempt to answer are: "What is the bridge between calling and completion?" "What are the necessary ingredients that will take us from awareness to fulfillment?" "How do we move from knowing what we're here to do to actually doing it?" My answer: you have to have an intimate relationship with the S-word.

Do You Know the Word?

Now, keep your seat belts on, readers. Hold your horses. The S-word I speak of is not the three-letter word that Salt-N-Pepa, Madonna, or Marvin Gaye sang about. It's not a four-letter curse word either. No, the word I'm thinking about is a ten-letter word called *submission.* Although equally controversial and avoided as the others in Christian contexts, submission is paramount to our re-presentation of Christ to the world. Sure, the term *submission* has been historically mishandled, theologically misused, and often taken out of biblical context— but just because it has been abused does not mean it should be avoided.

The truth is, purpose cannot be fulfilled without submission. The primary reason Jesus was successful in the earth is because He understood the S-word. Remember, it's one thing to be aware of what God has placed you here to do; it's another thing to submit to it. It's one thing to ask God for an answer to your prayer; it's another thing to submit to the answer He gives. It's one thing to ask for direction; it's another thing to follow the Spirit's leading when the arrow is pointing in the opposite direction of what you want. An awareness of purpose is one thing, but submission to that purpose is another.

Jesus is the ultimate example of a life completely satisfied in and submitted to God. In this chapter we will define submission and explore how Jesus submitted to the Father according to the Scriptures. We'll also investigate common myths that have caused us to become ambivalent toward the S-word. I believe that looking at each myth and comparing each one to the example of Christ will help us to reimagine submission so that ultimately we will have a more Christlike understanding of this bridge that is so vital to accomplishing our God-given purpose.

It's All Over the Place

Submission is everywhere in Scripture. If you haven't seen it lately, it might be because you have trained your eyes to gloss over it. But it only takes the consideration of a few verses for us to see its significance.

On the night before Jesus was crucified, He went to a garden called Gethsemane to pray. This was not a typical prayer meeting. It was a war of the wills. Jesus had to submit to the Father's orders even though His humanity did not desire to do so. When He dropped to His knees on that cold and silent night, His first sentence was not, "Hey, so let Me tell You how I want this to happen." He didn't pretend to be in control of His own life, even though He had the power to do what He wanted. Instead, He cried, "Abba, Father...everything is possible for you. Take this cup from me. Yet not what I will, but what you will" (Mark 14:36). That's submission at its best. In one prayer Jesus recognized the inner conflict between what He wanted and what the Father wanted—and still, He chose the Father. In plain English, He submitted.

Before this happened, Jesus has an encounter with the woman at the well in Samaria. His disciples urge Him to eat, but Jesus responds:

"I have food to eat that you know nothing about."

Then his disciples said to each other, "Could someone have brought him food?"

"My food," said Jesus, "is to do the will of him who sent me and to finish his work."

—JOHN 4:32–34

Two chapters later, Jesus says it again:

"For I have come down from heaven not to do my will but to do the will of him who sent me."

—JOHN 6:38

Submission teaches us that it is impossible to be like Christ and do life "our way." Jesus submitted His entire life to the Father, and because He did so, our sins are eternally forgiven. Because He submitted, our pasts no longer control us. Because He submitted, our names have been etched into the Lamb's Book of Life. We are beneficiaries of His submission, and when we respond in a similar fashion, we reflect Christ.

The adversary is aware of this fact, and for this reason he attempts to pervert our purpose by robbing us of the gift of submission. If he can't keep us from getting saved, then he will try to stop us from being submitted.

GET UNDER IT

What is submission? For some, it's a list of rules and regulations that authority figures such as higher officials or controlling parents enforce. For others, it's a traumatizing word that reminds them of slavery and violence. But according to Scripture, submission is the only way to serve God and live in community with elders, parents, children, spouses, and employers. Please note this. Highlight it. Circle it. Memorize it if you must. If we call ourselves Christians, then submission is the only way to live. It's not an option or a multiple-choice test. It is a requirement.

The prefix *sub* means "to go under or to get under." Therefore, like a submarine is underwater, so too should we be "under" the mission. In general, we have to make a conscious decision to serve under someone's mission, vision, or plan, and we must also decide not to resist or work against it. In a biblical sense, then, *submission* means "to get under the mission of God," and our goal as citizens of Christ is to carry out whatever role we have been given in order to ensure that the mission of God is accomplished by any means necessary.

When we think about submission in this way, it helps us understand how to live it out in the context of human relationships. For example, the Scripture says, "Wives submit to your own husbands" (Eph. 5:22–23, KJV), and most of us assume God is telling us to submit to a person. In fact, you are getting under a mission. Submission here does not mean wives should become enslaved to their spouses and do whatever their fallible counterparts ask them to do. Submission means a wife recognizes her husband has a God-given mission to lead, cover, and protect their family. Her role, then, is to support that vision and ensure the cohesion of her family by getting under that mission. A submitted wife must make a conscious decision not to work against her spouse. At the same time, a husband must have a mission that his wife can submit to. Husbands need to clearly define what the family mission is and be equally submitted to God as the wife is submitted to him. This is the only way submission will work, and this is exactly what Ephesians is calling us to live out.

It is impossible to get under a mission that doesn't exist. Husbands are not exempt from submission, and neither are singles, widows, divorcees, or any other type of person we can be. The same way wives ought to submit to their husbands, husbands must also be submitted to God. Everyone must be under the mission of God. In simple terms, the husband must receive His mission from the Lord and the wife from her husband. So when you think about it, every mission comes from the Lord. And when a husband's mission comes from God, it is easy for the wife to submit. Why? Because the branches of their life together stem directly from God, the vine.

Let's take another example of submission in Scripture. When Scripture advises us to submit to spiritual leadership, what does that mean? Hebrews 13:17 says, "Obey them that have the rule over you, and submit yourselves: for they watch for your souls, as they that must give account, that they may do it with joy, and not with grief: for that is unprofitable for you" (KJV). For starters, this verse doesn't mean you will lose your creative edge and unique voice if you submit. Submission has no losses, only gains! Submission to spiritual leadership recognizes that no tree grows without roots. It helps us understand our leader's mission, and it gives us a target to hit in the accomplishment of that mission. Submission reminds us we are not islands unto ourselves—that everything we do affects someone for better or for worse. The easiest way for you to flourish and grow is to be under your leader's mission, because one day you may need someone to be under yours!

Human relationships are guideposts for our spiritual relationship with God. The better we relate to others, the better we will be able to relate to God—and the better we relate to God, the better we can relate to others. When we get under God's mission, we are in essence saying, "I know You have a purpose for my life, and I don't want to get in Your way." We readily abandon our plans because we trust God is smarter than us.

Submitting to God is no easy task, but in order to be like Christ, we have to do it. Jesus says it this way: "Deny yourself, take up your cross daily and follow Me." (See Luke 9:23.) Failure to do so will leave us open to the lies, myths, and distortions of the enemy.

IT ALL STARTED IN THE GARDEN

So, let's think about how we got here. I'm not talking about how we got here in this chapter—I'm talking about our human existence and the condition of our wayward hearts. How did human beings end up so far away from God? It didn't all begin this way. So what transpired that interrupted eternal love and enjoyment with God? The easy answer would be sin. And that is correct. But how did sin edge its way into Adam's and Eve's hearts? I contend that sin came in through a few myths about submission. Let me explain what I mean.

The first man and woman, Adam and Eve, were triumphant and happy, but the opponent of our souls lured them into rebellion. With just a few words and gestures, he deceived Adam and Eve into settling for a relationship without lordship. This is important to notice because many of us have no problem with God until He challenges us to do something we don't want to do. It's not until He is our Lord that He can become our Savior, and until we accept that truth, we are just like Adam and Eve—satisfied with relationship in exchange for lordship.

Eve's actions in the Garden of Eden reveal an unfortunate reality that exists in our Christian context. Eve's primary sin was not that she ate from a forbidden tree; her primary sin was that she tried to dethrone her Creator. She wanted to become the god of her own life. She wanted to submit to nothing and have access to everything. In our postmodern Christian communities, Dallas Willard called this mind-set "vampire Christianity"—a kind of faith that wants Jesus's blood but nothing else.[2] These are Christians who say, "Forgive me, but don't tell me how to live my life." They cry, "Be my personal assistant and give me what I want, but let me live the way I want to live." Vampire Christians admit, "I need your help, God," but whenever God says something inconsistent with their bucket list, they want out. Like Eve, they will reject God's Word and do what they want to do in the name of blaming someone else.

I see four myths in the Adam and Eve narrative by which we must be careful not to be deceived. Here is what Eve's mistake with the serpent can teach us about submission.

1. The enemy gets Eve with the myth of restriction.

When Eve was told not to eat from the tree, she interpreted that commandment to mean punishment, not protection. In the same way, many of us are afraid of submission because we equate it with words such as *punishment, confinement,* or *imprisonment.* "The moment I have to submit to my parents," we say, "I know I will be grounded for coming home past curfew," or "I may not be able to go to the prom due to substandard grades." But the curfew is for your safety, and the grades are for your future success. Proms will come and go, but those grades will forever remain on your transcript! People who see submission as punitive do not understand the blessing behind things such as a speed limit. To fast drivers, speed limits restrict them from driving as fast as they want to go. But for those who are wise, speed limits keep you alive. The same is true with submission.

Submission is not a loss of freedom but protection of it. Too much of anything can become toxic and unhealthy. In the same way, the lack of boundaries can create an insatiable monster within you. What does that mean? It means that if you can't say no, then you aren't free. If every time your phone rings you stop what you are doing to satisfy the needs of someone distracting you from your goal, then you are bound by your inability to say no. Submission to God keeps us protected so we can keep our freedom. We must learn to say no to some things so we can experience life as God intended. Submission, then, is not control—it is protective custody.

2. The enemy gets Eve with the myth of identity.

To lure Eve into sin, the devil says, "For God knows that when you eat from it your eyes will be opened, and you will be like God, knowing good and evil" (Gen. 3:5). In other words, he plays on her identity. He confuses her understanding of what it means to be human and dupes her into believing that God was withholding some esoteric secret from her and Adam by prohibiting her from eating of the tree.

Often the same happens with us. We feel less than human when God doesn't show us the details of our lives when we want to know them. But our identities are wrapped up in and revealed by our submission to God. To put it plainly, submission is not a loss of identity; it is the discovery of it. Submission is a human decision to allow an eternal God—who knows all and sees all—to reveal and shape our true identities. It's only by submitting to our Creator that we can actually discover why He made us and who He made us to be.

Submission doesn't rob us of our identities; it helps us discover them. Philippians confirms this very truth about Jesus when it said He, "being in the form of God, thought it not robbery to be equal with God: but made himself of no reputation, and took upon him the form of a servant, and was made in the likeness of men: and being found in fashion as a man, he humbled himself, and became obedient unto death, even the death of the cross" (Phil. 2:6–8, KJV).

The point about submission and identity is as clear as a Windex mirror here! Jesus, who is God, submitted Himself to the will of the Father so much that He didn't even tell others who He was. He refused reputation and fanfare. He opted for the servant's garments and became obedient unto a brutal and unfair death—all in the name of submission. Jesus placed the mission over His ego. He knew who He was and didn't allow anyone around Him to convince Him out of His role. Someone who is unwilling to play his or her role is someone who doesn't know what role they were created to play.

Jesus knew His role and executed it effectively. His identity as Christ was wrapped in the persecution of His accusers and in the misrepresentation of His character. The more He submitted to God, the greater His identity emerged; the more we surrender, the more ours will also.

3. The enemy gets Eve with the myth of opinion.

Do you know someone who is so opinionated that they always have to add their two cents to the conversation? No matter what you are talking about, they will either disagree or nitpick about semantics just so they can be heard. Humans of all ages struggle with this need to be heard. We want our opinions to matter, and when we feel we have lost our voice, we scream from the mountaintop until someone acknowledges our presence.

Eve was no different. By eating from the tree she assumed her opinion and her interpretation of what God said was more important than what God actually said. The serpent preyed on her weakness by asking her, "Do you really think that's what God meant when He said that?" And like many of us, Eve took the bait. All she needed was one contradictory voice to push her into disobedience.

Particularly in America the convenience of an opinionated people is supported by our democracy. I personally love living in a democratic republic; however, the kingdom of God is not a democracy. In Jesus's day there were authoritarian kings and totalitarian systems that in no way accommodated differences of opinion. God's kingdom works in similar fashion. However, our King is a loving servant who wants what's best for us. He doesn't want us to be void of opinions; He simply knows we need to discipline them.

Submission is not the absence of one's opinion; it is the yielding up of it. In other words, submitting doesn't mean we can't think for ourselves or that we don't have a brain to make rational decisions. Rather, it means we recognize and accept our cognitive limitations. We are human beings, and on our smartest day we could never outsmart God. Our opinion pales in comparison. Our sophistication bows down to the sovereignty and omnipotence of our King. A submitted mind accepts that it does not know more than God and decides to deposit the greatest energy investing in kingdom principles. Instead of asking, "What do I think?," a submitted person will ask, "What does the Bible say?" He will investigate God's perspective (vis-à-vis the Bible) instead of expressing multiple views about the situation.

At the end of the day we do not belong to ourselves. We are God's ambassadors. We are His vessels. The excellency of the power of God is placed in us, but it doesn't belong to us. All power belongs to God. Therefore, our opinion is placed under His mission—at all times and in all contexts.

4. He gets Eve with the myth of happiness.

The devil deceives Eve into believing she and Adam are missing out on something. In his mind, eating the fruit from the tree will yield multiple streams of pleasure and satisfaction. It will make humans happy if they don't submit.

But *happiness* is an interesting word. It never gives

what it promises and always makes you pay more for what you want than you originally bargained. Submission is our protection from the myth of happiness. It is not a forfeiting of happiness but the discovery of true joy.

When you are truly submitted to God, His desires become your desires. You begin to want things you never wanted, and you detest things you thought you could never live without. You encounter real joy, which has nothing to do with monetary success or power and mobility; it is an inner peace that surpasses understanding. True joy makes you want to live longer and reach wider. It gives you the strength to endure what you cannot avoid.

Although submission is often presented in direct opposition to happiness, the truth is that serving under God's mission is the only place where humans can truly be fulfilled without the tax of sin debt. Human happiness produces an inferior and transient emotional being. Godly joy produces a woman or man of God who has learned, in whatever state they are in, to be content. Human happiness is always connected to external circumstances that are always desired but rarely achieved. As soon as you accomplish one thing, you will want another.

Submission to God reminds us of the big picture, and the big picture is that God wants you to have unspeakable joy. When we uncover these myths and expose the lies connected to freedom, opinion, identity, and happiness, we bump into a life filled with boundless opportunities to submit to God and enjoy Him forever.

JESUS RIGHTS THE WRONG

Jesus no doubt understood the importance and the blessing of submission, and this is why what worked with Eve did not work with Jesus. In Matthew 4 Jesus is led into the wilderness to be tempted by the devil. He is tempted to live according to appetite (how He feels), ego (what He thinks about Himself), and an alternative point of view than the one He's been given (new information).

However, Jesus models something for us in His response. He responds to the adversary each time by telling him, "It is written." In other words, although the devil made a case for different things that appealed to Jesus at the moment, the final authority concerning what was appropriate and inappropriate was not found in logic or opinion, but in the Word of God. The blessings of sub-mission come when we cross-examine our decisions next to the Scriptures. If the Bible says something different, then my job is not to debate or to try to reinterpret the Scripture to conform to my ways. My job is to submit myself to the Scripture. Why? Because the Scriptures are the standard of truth by which we are to live our lives. Jesus understood and submitted to this.

Notice that after Jesus was tempted to turn the stones into bread, He never said, "I don't want it." Of course He wanted to eat! Of course He was hungry. But His response was one of submission. He said, "It is written." In other words, Jesus knew that our appetites and feel-ings are not the final authority. It doesn't matter how strongly we feel about something, if our feelings are not consistent with the Scriptures, they are nothing more than feelings. No matter how many books we have read or how many scholars we know personally, if the conclusion of our facts contradicts the truth of our faith, then we must accept it as a beautifully decorated lie. Only the Word can stand as the truth—not our opinions, not our feelings, not our cravings, not our sophistication.

I know this is a difficult pill to swallow, but it is medicine for your soul! Make no mistake about it, friends: there will come a day when you will have to choose God's will over your wants. But re-presenting Christ means doing what is written over indulging in what is wanted.

Chapter 6

JESUS and GENEROSITY

*Either the key to a man's wallet is in his
heart, or the key to a man's heart is in his
wallet. So, unless you express your charity,
you are locked inside your greed.*[1]
—NOAH benSHEA

ONE OF MY core passions in ministry is discipleship. More than anything else I am most fulfilled when learning and helping others learn to
live like Jesus. I'm sure you know that by now, given the
title of this book and the content of each chapter, but
my love for discipleship is more than a personal passion.
I believe it is a biblical mandate. Disciple making isn't
some ornamental accessory. It isn't the extra thing we do
at church. It is the core of Christianity. Everything else is
ornamental. The church can live without a building or a
website, as outrageous as that may seem in the Western
world, but we cannot function without discipleship. A
church that fails to disciple is not a church at all—it may
be a religious organization, an elitist club, or a spiritual
retreat center, but it is not the church that Jesus built.

Listen to the words of Jesus written in Matthew 28:19–20:

> Therefore go and make disciples of all nations, baptizing them in the name of the Father and of the Son and of the Holy Spirit, and teaching them to obey everything I have commanded you. And surely I am with you always, to the very end of the age.

Some have never read this verse before, while others have heard it so many times it has lost its potency. I pray that the Holy Spirit will re-present this verse to you in a fresh way. Imagine Christ talking directly to you: *Therefore go and make disciples of all nations, baptizing them in the name of the Father and of the Son and of the Holy Spirit, and teaching them to obey everything I have commanded you. And surely I am with you always, to the very end of the age.*

Those two sentences encapsulate the essence of the kingdom life. Each verb is a clue that hints at Jesus's core values: *go, make, baptize, teach,* and *obey.* To *go* means to move. It seems obvious, I'm sure, but this word requires emphasis. Going means leaving. Moving. Stepping out. We can't expect the world to knock on our door. We can't expect our unchurched family members to invite themselves to Family and Friends Day. We must go—travel, leave our comfortable habitations, and live out the gospel message of Jesus Christ. If we don't, the mission will not be accomplished.

The word *make* implies a significant and sometimes arduous process that is required in order to turn the raw materials of our human frailties into the righteous individuals we are all called to be. Sanctification does not happen overnight, and it also requires some intentionality on our part. There are some things we must put off and some traits we must put on. No one gets better at anything by accident. It's a process.

Baptizing deals with a submersion of sorts—a death to the old nature and a rising with Christ in a new and fresh way. As a disciple, baptism is and should always be an important symbol in the Christian faith. A seed must be buried in the ground before the harvest of its fruit can spring forth. In the same way, we must be buried with Christ as Romans 6:4 suggests: "Therefore we are buried with him by baptism into death: that like as Christ was raised up from the dead by the glory of the Father, even so we also should walk in newness of life" (KJV).

Teach is one of my favorite words. Jesus includes it in the Great Commission to remind us of the importance of impartation and instruction. Disciples don't become disciples through osmosis. Disciples are not disciples because they wear the right clothes or boast an affiliation to a particular denomination or nondenomination. Disciples become disciples when they are taught. We are taught how to be like Christ. We are taught how to think like Christ. We are taught how to behave like Christ, and the more we learn how to be, the better we will become at obeying God.

Speaking of which, *obey* is the final verb in this scripture. I believe it's mentioned last because when the previous four are intentionally pursued, obedience becomes second nature. When a Christian knows what to obey, why to obey it, and most importantly, who empowers us to obey, then obedience is an achievable goal as opposed to an unrealistic expectation.

On the basis of these five verbs alone, we see proof that Jesus came to do more than provide us with a hall pass to heaven. He came to lead us on earth. As a matter of fact, most of Jesus's teaching was focused on how to survive and thrive on earth, not how to get to heaven. Please don't mishear me. I'm not saying heaven is not significant or important. I'm simply saying Jesus talked and taught more about our present life than the afterlife.

In essence, Jesus wants to show us how to live life the King's way. And when I say life, I mean every area of it. There is nothing that impacts our lives that He is not deeply concerned with. However, if we would all be honest, we have some areas where we are not as open to His teaching. We have some "off-limits" areas we would prefer Jesus wouldn't talk about. We have these areas figured out, right? No need for Jesus to talk about certain spaces and places in our lives because we're good, right? Wrong. Jesus wants to instruct us and lead us in every single area. An adage comes to mind that I believe is true: Jesus is Lord of all, or He isn't Lord at all. This means we should give Him access to instruct us in every area of our lives, including the areas that have historically been off-limits.

And what is the number one off-limits area that needs deconstruction in most of our lives? Survey says: money.

MONEY MADNESS

Many people believe money has nothing to do with spirituality. But the Bible would suggest otherwise. In the Gospels, Jesus tells at least thirty-eight parables, and of those thirty-eight, sixteen are about money or use money as an example to teach us about something else. That means almost half of Jesus's messages are preoccupied with the subject we want to control: money. Why? I imagine it's because Jesus knows the real issue is not our desire for economic success but the distraction of idolatry.

Yes—idolatry.

Anything that steals our devotion and affection from God is an idol. Idols are alluring. Idols are attractive. They promise to provide what only God can give. Idols offer happiness without holiness, but it's only an illusion. Idols promise security without salvation, but that too is only an illusion. Idols pretend to give esteem without establishment, and in the end they always leave us more broken than when they found us.

Jesus knows that idolatry is at the heart of money madness. Very often we become slaves to money without realizing it. Financial gain becomes more important than God. We wake up thinking about it, running toward it, obsessed by it, and overwhelmed because of it.

But how did Jesus view money? What does He say in the Scriptures about the relationship between faith and finances? How can we make sure that the blessing of generosity never turns into a curse called greed? When the rubber meets the road, Jesus was generous. He was generous with His greatest asset and resource, which was His life. This may sound blunt, but I believe it's true: *If we aren't generous, then we aren't like Jesus.* What we do with our lives and our resources matters.

MONEY MATTERS

Jesus seems to suggest quite strongly that money matters. How we value it matters, how much we love it matters, and how we use it matters. Luke 16:9–15 reveals these concerns clearly and succinctly:

> "I tell you, use worldly wealth to gain friends for yourselves, so that when it is gone, you will be welcomed into eternal dwellings.
>
> "Whoever can be trusted with very little can also be trusted with much, and whoever is dishonest with very little will also be dishonest with much. So if you have not been trustworthy in handling worldly wealth, who will trust you with true riches? And if you have not been trustworthy with someone else's property, who will give you property of your own?
>
> "No one can serve two masters. Either you will hate the one and love the other, or you will be devoted to the one and despise the other. You cannot serve both God and money."
>
> The Pharisees, who loved money, heard all this and were sneering at Jesus. He said to them, "You are the ones who justify yourselves in the eyes of others, but God knows your hearts. What people value highly is detestable in God's sight."

Values reveal a person's view of a thing. If you value your family, then your view is that they are more important to you than working countless hours—so if you need to, you will cut down your work hours to spend time with those you value. Similarly, how we value money tells others how we view it. Money should never be seen as a source. A biblical view of money is that it's simply a resource.

If you read Luke 16 in its entirety, it will help you to see this point more clearly. There are a rich man and a manager in the parable. The manager has been accused of wasting the rich man's possessions, but the problem is, those riches aren't his to waste! The manager isn't the owner of the riches. His job is simply to oversee someone else's abundance. Later, when the rich man asks the manager to give an account of his management, the manager realizes what he squandered and mismanaged never belonged to him in the first place.

How does that relate to us? First of all, God is responsible for everything we own. The earth is the Lord's and the fullness thereof. Our success does not come from our hard work alone, but from a generous and gracious God who provides us with skill sets and opportunities we can leverage into provision.

When Jesus tells this parable to His listeners, He advises them not to compromise their relationships with the God who "hired them" by using money against the God who provided it. This is the equivalent of a friend buying a gift for another friend, only for the recipient of that gift to abandon the giver of the gift for the gift itself. The receiver has overlooked the fact that the source of her joy did not come from the gift but from the relationship cultivated with the friend she just abandoned. When we learn to view money the way Jesus valued it, we won't disobey God to get it or keep it. Money matters, but it shouldn't matter more than our relationships with God.

Worldly Wealth vs. True Riches

Jesus doesn't even see money as true riches. Luke 16:11 says, "So if you have not been trustworthy in handling worldly wealth, who will trust you with *true* riches?" (emphasis added). Did you notice the distinction between worldly wealth and true riches? Jesus doesn't even place them in the same category because money is a gauge, not a god. What we do with worldly wealth only foreshadows how we will handle true riches. Money is not the be-all, end-all of our human existence, and Jesus's juxtaposition in this verse proves that.

What if true riches were never meant to be determined by quantifiable dollars and cents but by the relationships we foster, the influence we've been given, or the favor God grants us to access what money cannot? All of us have encountered, at one point or another, a time when we needed a miracle that money could not fix. But knowing the right person or having the right job or driving on the right street allowed us access into true riches.

In 2010 *Forbes* estimated the net worth of Steve Jobs, cofounder and CEO of Apple Inc., at $8.3 billion, but in 2003 he was diagnosed with a terminal illness that worldly riches could not fix. His life ended at the vibrant age of fifty-six due to pancreatic cancer. I wonder how your perception of money would change if this happened to you and you were forced to consider the true riches around you: the inner peace you have when your child comes home safely from school; the indescribable joy you experience after you say "I do"; the memories shared between loved ones who have died; the sound of your baby saying *mama* or *dada* for the first time. These are what Jesus calls true riches.

Money is a resource, not our source. Money is a gauge, not a god. And money is a tool, not a treasure. Money should be a tool used wisely, not a treasure to be hoarded. And the same way our earthly relationships help us develop a better relationship with God, money is a tool that prepares us for eternity. As such, Jesus teaches that we are to use the tool wisely because anything that is used outside of its intended purpose can lead to its abuse. As disciples we can value the tool of money without worshipping it as a treasure. Money helps us worship and serve God. It helps us make connections with people and aid the least of these. We should use it as a tool to honor God, care for our families, and serve those in need. When we do, we position ourselves for an even greater investment in heaven.

How Much Do You Love Money?

I want to be clear: I am in no way suggesting money is not necessary or important. I don't believe that is consistent with the teachings of Jesus. Jesus seemed to have no issue with money. The issue is the place it holds in our lives. Do we love it more than God? God has no issue with you having money. God's issue is, does money have you? Money is amoral. In other words, it has no moral value in and of itself. The hands that manage the money determine its morality. A philanthropist might use money to build shelters and fund schools. A terrorist can use it to design bombs and construct weapons. One person might be rich and righteous; the other might be poor and wicked. The real issue is a heart issue.

How much do you love money? Do you control it, or does it control you? Are you chasing after it, or does it somehow chase after you? Do you work to earn as much as possible, or are you working because you enjoy what you do? Jesus says in Matthew 6:21, "For where your treasure is, there your heart will be also." This doesn't mean we should not value money. In fact, I believe God wants us to have as much money as our character can handle—as long as money is not loved more than Him.

God cautions us not to honor anything more than we honor Him. He warns us not to be more devoted to getting it than we are committed to getting to Him. This is seen all throughout Scripture, but most vividly in Malachi, when God says to Israel, "'A son honors his father, and a slave his master. If I am a father, where is the honor due me? If I am a master, where is the respect due me?' says the LORD Almighty" (Mal. 1:6).

Money is a heart matter and an honor issue. What we honor, we reverence; and what we reverence, we worship. If we stop honoring God to reverence what we deem to be another more suitable candidate—in this case, money—we have turned our hearts toward the gift and not the Giver. We honor work but not God. We honor the image of success but not the one who made us in His image.

We can't serve God and money. The call to discipleship is a call to choose—not to choose one or the other but one *over* the other. It's only when we see it from this vantage point that we can use money the way God intended.

How Do You Use Money?

Money is a mirror. That's right—it's a mirror. It's a mirror that reflects and reveals our priorities and our values.

This is why Jesus not only teaches the importance of seeing money biblically but also managing it appropriately. In other words, Jesus isn't just concerned with how we see money or how we make it. He is equally interested in what we do with it. This is the essence of stewardship. It is the use of money and the way we dispense or deposit it that measures our stewardship.

In Matthew 25:14–30 Jesus paints a descriptive portrait of what poor stewardship and productive stewardship look like:

> Again, it will be like a man going on a journey, who called his servants and entrusted his wealth to them. To one he gave five bags of gold, to another two bags, and to another one bag, each according to his ability. Then he went on his journey. The man who had received five bags of gold went at once and put his money to work and gained five bags more. So also, the one with two bags of gold gained two more. But the man who had received one bag went off, dug a hole in the ground and hid his master's money.
>
> After a long time the master of those servants returned and settled accounts with them. The man who had received five bags of gold brought the other five. "Master," he said, "you entrusted me with five bags of gold. See, I have gained five more."
>
> His master replied, "Well done, good and faithful servant! You have been faithful with a few things; I will put you in charge of many things. Come and share your master's happiness!"
>
> The man with two bags of gold also came.

"Master," he said, "you entrusted me with two bags of gold; see, I have gained two more."

His master replied, "Well done, good and faithful servant! You have been faithful with a few things; I will put you in charge of many things. Come and share your master's happiness!"

Then the man who had received one bag of gold came. "Master," he said, "I knew that you are a hard man, harvesting where you have not sown and gathering where you have not scattered seed. So I was afraid and went out and hid your gold in the ground. See, here is what belongs to you."

His master replied, "You wicked, lazy servant! So you knew that I harvest where I have not sown and gather where I have not scattered seed? Well then, you should have put my money on deposit with the bankers, so that when I returned I would have received it back with interest.

"So take the bag of gold from him and give it to the one who has ten bags. For whoever has will be given more, and they will have an abundance. Whoever does not have, even what they have will be taken from them. And throw that worthless servant outside, into the darkness, where there will be weeping and gnashing of teeth."

Just like the parable told in Luke 16 about the rich man and his manager, this parable reminds us that all we have comes from God. God is the "man going on a journey" who will come back to see how we have managed what He has given us. God blessed each of us with a mind, and He tells us how to manage it. He has given us a body, and He tells us how to manage it. It is God who makes it possible for us to obtain resources, and He tells us how we should manage them. It's a bit inconsistent to say God can tell me what to do with my body and my mind but not my resources, isn't it? Being a disciple means giving it all to Him, and if we properly manage what He gives, then it will work for our benefit. If we mismanage money, it will work for our detriment.

A good manager of resources will manage faithfully and consistently. The master in this parable calls the first two servants "good and faithful." Good management includes knowing how much one has and knowing where it should go. Faithful management involves spending wisely. Poor stewardship will always hide money in the dirt. The poor steward will waste money on things that don't matter. Good stewardship, on the other hand, will save for winter seasons while simultaneously investing in the future.

Saving is not burying. When you save money, you invest intentionally in your future gains. But when you squander or selfishly hide your money, it will never yield a significant profit for you. Ants even know this, according to Proverbs: "Go to the ant, you sluggard; consider its ways and be wise! It has no commander, no overseer or ruler, yet it stores its provisions in summer and gathers its food at harvest" (Prov. 6:6–8).

A good manager of resources is one who lives modestly. This means your lifestyle should be in proportion to the "bags of gold" God has given you. Remember, to one person, God gave five bags. To another, God gave two. The third man was given one bag. Modest living means living on your level without apology or comparison. Oftentimes people who live above their means are battling discontentment and insecurity. Beware of what one

Christian leader calls the "comparison trap," the impulse to be greater than someone whose lifestyle is different than yours. This kind of thinking is an ungodly temptation motivated by the false god of worldly wealth.

Good managers enjoy life and spend money to do so, but they do not live as if high seasons never end. They never make long-term commitments based on a bonus. The same way seasons change with regard to the weather, seasons change with our finances as well. Good stewards must predict and prepare for the season that is soon to come while enjoying the current season they are in.

It is only when we are good and wise managers that we can model generosity as Jesus did. Generous giving is easy to those who practice generous living. In Mark 12 Jesus sat down and watched people putting money into the offering basket. Many gave out of abundance, but the poor widow gave out of her generosity. You remember the story, right? Her two coins, says Jesus, were of more value than all the other contributions that day.

Giving generously is not about a certain amount. It's about the discipline to remain consistent and the motivation that inspires that consistency. It requires a daily decision to choose God over money, and it isn't always easy—but it is certainly the way Jesus taught us to view money. Money is complicated. It's a blessing to have and an even greater blessing to give away. At the same time, the love of money is the root of all evil. When our hearts yearn for money more than they yearn for God, we must reevaluate our riches and seek God's Word for direction.

Despite the distractions of popular culture and the poor decisions made by corrupt and avaricious leaders—both in the church and outside of it—Jesus is calling us to renovate our minds about money. If we are going to be like Him in every aspect of our lives, then we must do more than merely wrestle with this idol. We must tear it down completely and live lives of radical generosity! I'm reminded of the words of Patti Digh, who once said, "Being generous often consists of simply extending a hand."[2] Jesus did it for us, and may God grant us the wisdom and wherewithal to do it for others.

Chapter 7

JESUS and SPIRITUAL DISCIPLINES

*I must take care above all that I culti-
vate communion with Christ, for though that
can never be the basis of my peace—mark
that—yet it will be the channel of it.*[1]
—CHARLES SPURGEON

EVER SINCE I was a child, I've admired Michael
Jordan. At one time, I wanted to do everything
Mike did. I wanted to wear my shorts like he wore
his. I wanted to stick out my tongue like he did. Mike
was my hero. Whatever I had to do, I would do it, because
ultimately I wanted to play like Mike on the basketball
court.

Suffice it to say, God had another plan for me. I
wouldn't be writing this book if I had succeeded! But if
I wanted to be like Mike, it would be illogical for me to
expect to do what Michael Jordan did publicly without
practicing the way he did privately. It would be unrealistic of me to want the glamour of his success without
enduring the rigor of his preparation.

Most wouldn't believe it now, but Michael Jordan was

not a precocious all-star athlete. He was no prodigy from birth. In high school he was cut from the varsity basketball team during his sophomore year. He wasn't the most popular kid, and older boys made fun of him for sticking out his tongue during games. The odds were completely against him, but he had unbelievable drive and resilience. His competitive edge was unprecedented. He worked in the cold, in the heat, and during the off-seasons. His goal was to perfect his game, and through private practice he became a public phenomenon. He disciplined himself, and through his discipline and preparation he became one of the greatest athletes of all time.

Personally I was inspired by his on-court play but never emulated his personal practices. Therefore, I couldn't perform like Mike in public because I didn't do what Mike did in private.

What Michael Jordan is to basketball, Jesus is to life. He is unequivocally and undeniably the greatest of all time. His name is the most famous name on the planet. Time is divided based on His birth. The book about Him, the Bible, is the best-selling book of all time. Jesus is the greatest, and many of us want to be like Him.

However, just as was the case with Mike, there is no way we can be like Jesus in public without emulating what He did in private. We must do more than admire His public performance; we must investigate His private life. To be like Him, we have to study what He did and mimic His pattern. If He prayed, we should pray. If He fasted, we should fast. If He served, we must serve. All of these private practices produced a public phenomenon in the person of Jesus Christ because, in a word, Jesus was *disciplined*. Likewise, in order to do what Jesus did and to be who Jesus was, we must be willing to embrace the spiritual disciplines.

While discipline is often overlooked, it is an extremely important part of Jesus's character. At the same time, I must be clear: I am not pointing this out to make an argument for a life of regimented asceticism. Nor I am advocating a theology of works-righteousness. I believe Jesus modeled a consistent pattern of spiritual disciplines during His earthly ministry—and if Jesus, who is God, had to be disciplined, then how much more should we mere mortals do the same?

Scripture makes it plain in 1 Timothy 4:7: "Have nothing to do with godless myths and old wives' tales; rather, train yourself to be godly." The King James Version says, "Exercise thyself rather unto godliness." That word *exercise* is transliterated in the Greek as *gymnasia*, which is where the word *gymnasium* comes from. Why is this important? Because Paul is saying, "If you're going to be godly, then it's going to take a spiritual workout in the gym of discipline." We will never be strong in our faith until we exercise certain muscles on a consistent basis. Godliness won't happen simply because you want it. It will happen because you willed it.

The same way we go to the gym to exercise our natural bodies, we must go to the Father, like Jesus did, to exercise our spiritual bodies. It is this kind of practice that does not make you perfect, but it will make you better. In this chapter I want to consider a few biblical passages to highlight five spiritual disciplines that are ubiquitous in the life of Jesus. These fabulous five include *prayer, fasting, worship,* the *studying of Scripture,* and *service.*

Prayer

Let's start off with a few self-evaluation questions. Please answer them as honestly as possible: How often do you pray? When you pray, what do you say? Is prayer an ecclesial mandate or a guilty pleasure? Do you enjoy it as much as Jesus did, or does it feel like a chore?

Certainly Jesus placed a high priority on prayer, but why? What did prayer do for Him that helped Him to live a more disciplined life? Here are a few verses that track Jesus's prayer life:

> About eight days after Jesus said this, he took Peter, John and James with him and went up onto a mountain to pray. As he was praying, the appearance of his face changed, and his clothes became as bright as a flash of lightning.
> —Luke 9:28–29

> Very early in the morning, while it was still dark, Jesus got up, left the house and went off to a solitary place, where he prayed.
> —Mark 1:35

> Immediately Jesus made the disciples get into the boat and go on ahead of him to the other side, while he dismissed the crowd. After he had dismissed them, he went up on a mountainside by himself to pray. Later that night, he was there alone, and the boat was already a considerable distance from land, buffeted by the waves because the wind was against it.

Shortly before dawn Jesus went out to them, walking on the lake.

—MATTHEW 14:22–25

According to Luke 9:29, prayer changes our outlook. It also changes what we look like to others. What an amazing moment in Scripture this passage portrays! As Jesus is praying, He transfigures in front of His disciples. He didn't change clothes or wave a magic wand, but their perception of His appearance changed the moment He prayed. In the same way, when you pray, change is inevitable. The conditions may not change. The circumstances will probably remain the same. But prayer changes how you respond to crisis. It changes how people see you in crisis. Without prayer, nothing transfigures.

Mark 1:35 reveals that prayer was such a priority to Christ that He removed Himself from the noise of life in order to do it with intention. I'm sure many of us pray while driving or pray while getting the kids ready for school, but how often do you retreat intentionally in order to focus on God and God alone? Prayer is so easy to do but so difficult to maintain. In order to witness its fruit, you have to concentrate your energy and remove yourself from the noise of life.

Jesus withdrew Himself frequently to be refreshed in the presence of God. In like manner the discipline of prayer helps you to be refreshed and to refresh things around you. Let me give you an example. If you use the Internet to read the news, you know how important it is to refresh the page, because the page you visited three hours ago will have new information made available throughout the day. But if you never click on that small circular icon otherwise known as the refresh button, you won't see any new and urgent information.

The beauty of prayer is the refreshing it brings. Prayer gives us a current update on the outlook of life's cares. If we do not enter into God's presence with intentional focus and concentration, we may be living with expired data. In prayer God whispers the hidden jewels of revelation into your ear. That's where business ideas come from. That's where you get the hunch to drive to one store instead of the other. That's when you are transformed in such a way that others know you've been with God just by your countenance and interaction with them.

Prayer causes you to rise above life's dismal and depressing waters. It helps you to see the world from the angle of heaven. Remember in Matthew 14 when Jesus walks on the water? Peter asks if he can come, and Jesus says one word: "Come." The request Peter made to Jesus—who is God—was a prayer. One sentence enabled Peter to walk on top of that which others had drowned in.

What if I told you God wants to increase your discipline of prayer not to bore you but to enable you? God doesn't want to restrict you. He wants to empower you! Furthermore, He wants to elevate your perspective above a situation others are drowning in.

Prayer also helps you to get to the same destination while taking an alternative route. Remember, the disciples in Matthew 14 had to row to get to where they were going in the lake, but after Jesus prayed, He walked there. Prayer makes the process so much easier. Some people row; some people walk. Some people interview, while others can write a check directly from their account.

When you pray, God allows you to take an alternative route and still arrive at the proper destination on time.

Prayer will redeem lost time. The text of Matthew 14 proves it. Jesus had sent the disciples ahead of Him. They left before He did, but He still caught up with them. In the same manner, prayer will help you to catch up. Even when you feel you have fallen behind schedule, when you pray, God discloses divine strategies to get you back in the place you belong.

Prayer is nonnegotiable. It's a catalyst for the cultivation of intimacy with God. If you want to be close to anyone, you have to talk to him or her. With God, the same rule applies. The benefit of intimacy is that you will be able to hear better because you are closer. Prayer brings you closer to God in such a way that it amplifies His voice by bringing down your voice. It's hard to make sense of what someone is saying when we are so far from them they have to yell to be heard. But when we get close enough to hear God, we are positioned to receive counsel from Him.

Ultimately prayer puts us in a position to receive divine counsel. We have all faced dilemmas where we needed God's help. We needed divine counsel, and Isaiah 9:6 says that Jesus is a wonderful counselor. But how can you receive counsel from Him unless you visit His office? Prayer is that office where Jesus sits with us, nods His head, and allows us to lie down on the couch. He has enough tissues for the whole world to cry on Him, and yet He cares enough about you to focus on you as if you are an only child. Sometimes the only counsel we need is the counsel we don't have to pay for. Prayer is a free spiritual service that allows you to bring all of your concerns to the wonderful counselor Himself.

FASTING

Prior to His public ministry Jesus spent forty days fasting. And of the five disciplines we will discuss, I perceive fasting may be the most challenging of them all. If you grew up like me, you love food! Food is, indeed, a gift from God. He provided it for our replenishment, but not for our diminishment. And whenever food messes up our faith, we've got a problem. Whenever the obsession to satisfy our stomachs becomes greater than the need to satisfy our Savior, then God leaves it to us to fast.

Tony Evans defines fasting as "the deliberate abstinence from some form of physical gratification...to achieve a greater spiritual goal."[2] I love this definition because it clarifies the purpose of the fast: to obtain a spiritual goal. This slight nuance is what distinguishes the discipline of fasting from mere abstinence. There are a number of ways to fast and various types of fasts. For example, it is possible to fast from pleasures such as social media, the Internet, sex, or any activity that brings gratification and satisfaction. However, I have chosen to focus on fasting from food because it is generally the most common type of fast and the type of fast Jesus practiced.

Also, I'd like to discuss three benefits to fasting that we see in the life Jesus modeled on earth.

Benefit #1: Fasting clears the mental and spiritual clutter.

I'm sure you know a few hoarders. Hoarders never throw anything away. They don't call their mess *clutter* because they always think they have their "organized chaos" under control. But if you go into their closets or garages, it's virtually impossible to see what is in the rooms. You can hurt yourself because there's too much stuff in one space. And when you refuse to clean it, it only gets worse.

When we fast, we clean out the clutter in our minds and hearts. Just as cleaning becomes all the more inconvenient and difficult when things pile up, our hearts becomes harder and harder the longer we prolong the cleansing process. Imagine what our spiritual closets can look like when we live a life of discipleship without the discipline of fasting. Prayer, the study of Scripture, and service are extremely important, but fasting has a unique and distinctive impact. It arrests the appetites of our flesh and heightens our spiritual senses to the degree that we are able to see the clutter in ways that we may not be able to see without the spiritual focus that fasting brings. Fasting, in a way that is different from any other spiritual discipline, teaches us to deny our desires over consistent periods of time. Fasting will not be an easy thing to embrace at first. But when you do it, you will experience undeniable results.

If you're anything like me, it's not until I clean something that I find valuable things I had been looking for. That's why God wants so desperately for you to embrace fasting. There are precious answers in the spiritual closet, waiting on you to take a time-out from life. God can't give you more until you clear out the unnecessary clutter in your life.

Benefit #2: Fasting increases our spiritual sensitivity.

Jentezen Franklin asserts, "Fasting is not a requirement; it is a choice. It is a vow you choose to make to pursue God on a deeper level."[3] For some of us, fasting would be easier to do if God forced us to do it. But the difficult part about this discipline is that you won't be excommunicated from heaven if you don't fast. There is no legalistic mandate forcing you to do it—or else.

All of the disciplines in this chapter are, in truth, voluntary acts of surrender, but fasting is unique to our human experience. Prayer arguably takes only a few moments of our day but doesn't inconvenience our tummies. Reading the Word can be done on the treadmill or during a lunch break. Service and worship can happen on a Sunday morning in church. But fasting leaves you longing for and yearning for fulfillment for an extended period of time. It's impossible to fast and not know it. Your stomach will begin to growl. Your body will begin to ache. What's funny is that on days when you're not fasting, you can go hours without eating. But when you determine to get closer to God through fasting, every fast-food restaurant comes to mind. Grocery sales increase in abundance when you're on a fast. It seems as if everyone is choosing to invite you to lunch on the day or week you're fasting. This is the only discipline that leaves you empty in order to make you full.

Similar to those among us who cannot hear, see, or smell, studies show that other senses become stronger when one sense is inactive. In other words, if I can't see because I have been diagnosed as blind, my hearing increases exponentially. An amazing strength and sensitivity rises up when another part of us dies. In the same way, when we resist eating, our flesh may long for fulfillment, but our spiritual being becomes more sensitive to the voice of God. Perhaps this is why Jesus could cast out demons His disciples could not:

> When they came to the crowd, a man came up to Jesus, falling on his knees before Him and saying, "Lord, have mercy on my son, for he is a lunatic and is very ill; for he often falls into the fire and often into the water. I brought him to Your disciples, and they could not cure him." And Jesus answered and said, "You unbelieving and perverted generation, how long shall I be with you? How long shall I put up with you? Bring him here to Me." And Jesus rebuked him, and the demon came out of him, and the boy was cured at once.
>
> Then the disciples came to Jesus privately and said, "Why could we not drive it out?" And He said to them, "Because of the littleness of your faith; for truly I say to you, if you have faith the size of a mustard seed, you will say to this mountain, 'Move from here to there,' and it will move; and nothing will be impossible to you. *[But this kind does not go out except by prayer and fasting."]*
> —Matthew 17:14–21, nas, emphasis added

The sensitivity Jesus fostered through fasting may have helped Him differentiate a supernatural stronghold from a natural disability. Notice that when Jesus answers the disciples, He doesn't address their commitment. He addresses their faith. The disciples had been loyal. They knew all of the right words to say. They sat under Jesus and had studied Him and His ways to a science. But they couldn't produce His power without the discipline of fasting. Their salvation was intact, but their sensitivity was off. When we fast, we become more sensitive to ourselves, to people around us, and most importantly, to God.

There is another appropriate example of this in Acts 13. Verse 2 suggests that the apostles were worshipping and fasting, and while they were doing so the Holy Spirit spoke and instructed them to set aside Paul and Barnabas for the work of ministry. Paul was already aware that he was called to ministry based on an experience he had on his way to Damascus in Acts 9. Therefore, the purpose of this reiteration of his calling was to confirm it was the right time for him to carry it out. The very next verse says that the apostles laid hands on Paul and Barnabas and sent them out. Please notice that they received this clarity regarding Paul's calling while they were fasting. I don't believe this is a coincidence. I believe their time of fasting helped increase their spiritual sensitivity so they were able to accurately discern the proper time to engage in ministry. Just as fasting served them in that way, it can also increase our sensitivity so that we can receive clear direction from God.

Benefit #3: Fasting provides us with a degree of intimacy with God.

I want to make sure that you are clear that when it comes to fasting and other spiritual disciplines, they all work in concert with one another. In Acts 13 the apostles were *worshipping and fasting* when the Holy Spirit spoke to them about Paul and Barnabas. However, one powerful partnership that fosters great intimacy with God is fasting and prayer. Jesus mentioned this partnership in Matthew 17 when He informed the disciples that certain stubborn situations are only removed by *fasting and prayer.* Prayer and fasting is a powerful and potent combination that pushes us closer to God. Fasting helps us detox from the carnal patterns that clutter our focus and ruin our vision. We pray so our fasting doesn't turn into a horrible form of dieting. Fasting without prayer is voluntary starvation. In order to reap the benefits of this discipline, you have to create new ways to pray with the end goal being to get closer to Jesus, and fasting aids us in doing so. Let nothing come between your intimacy with God.

SCRIPTURE READING

Jesus was clearly a student of the Scriptures. His vast knowledge of them communicates we too should make the study of Scripture a priority. Often when Jesus was questioned by people or tempted by Satan, He would respond with these words: "It is written." His accusers could not trip Him up because He committed Himself to speaking in the language of His Father. He always prized what the Father said over what He wanted to do. In like manner, if we are going to be like Jesus, we have to cultivate a disciplined life in the area of Scripture reading.

Is the reading of Scripture a part of your daily routine? When you read it, do you read to understand or do you read to finish? Do you read for your head or for your heart? Ritual without comprehension, purpose, or intentionality will only blur the lines between information and transformation. Jesus didn't approach the Scriptures this way. The Word was bread to Him. It fed His soul and helped Him to survive the hunger pangs of temptation. I love that when Jesus is tempted by the devil and he asks Jesus to turn the stone into bread, Jesus never says, "I don't want bread." He just responds, "It is written: man shall not live by bread alone." Here we see that Jesus placed the Word over His wants. He was hungry. He had been fasting for forty days. But His discipline allowed His spirit to say no to something His flesh had been craving and longing for. The more time you spend with God in His Word, the more strength you too will have to say no to things you really want to say yes to. The power to resist only comes from God through His Word.

When we buy electronic gadgets from the store, they often come with a manual that informs us how to get the most out of our purchase. The manual tells us how to use it, how to protect it, and how to care for it. These manuals are written by manufacturers because they are aware of the gadget's original purpose. The Bible works the same way. The Scriptures are like an operation manual for human life, and God's words help us learn from the lives of others on how to live as He, our Creator, intended. Like the gadget manual, the Bible teaches us how to use, protect, and care for our lives. When we don't read it, we are building a life without having to read the manual. We have a great tool but lack the know-how to enjoy its fullest purpose. It's hard to live out what we don't know. So we turn to the Scriptures as food for the soul.

> Like newborn babies, crave pure spiritual milk, so
> that by it you may grow up in your salvation, now
> that you have tasted that the Lord is good.
> —1 PETER 2:2–3

As babies, it is impossible to grow without the nutrition that comes from milk. As you grow older, the same milk that was used to develop you is now strengthening your muscles. The more strength you have, the more weight you can carry. So reading the Word is more about helping you to carry the weight of your life and less about doing it so others can notice you.

It's impossible to read the Scriptures and not grow up. Each time you read the Scriptures, they will help you to grow in salvation. Most certainly, you will begin to see life in a different way. Studying the Scriptures also impacts us by giving us nourishment from a spiritual perspective. Each time you commit to reading the Word, you gain the spiritual energy and strength to live like Christ.

The more I see how Jesus interpreted Scripture, the more I recognize the need to not just talk about Scripture reading here, but also to take a moment to discuss Scripture interpretation. Very often Jesus had to correct the practices of the religious leaders of His day as a result of them misinterpreting the meaning of Scripture. Second Timothy 2:15 calls this "rightly dividing the word of truth" (KJV).

Let's face it: Many wars have started because of misreadings of Scripture. Many lives have been abused because someone took one scripture out of context or decided to make the Bible say something God never meant when it was written. For that reason, it's important not only to read the Scriptures but also to know *how* to read them. I want to encourage you to develop a regimen of studying the Scriptures with humility, in honor, and with a hermeneutic of love.

By humility, I mean we never leave the posture of a student when we study God's Word. Even if we are teachers of the Word, we are and should always be students first. When we operate with this paradigm, it reduces the likelihood of our arrogantly approaching the Bible in ways that lead to us leaving with our own conclusions instead of God's. We must resist the temptation to read God's Word through our own logic and desires. In other words—again—God is smarter than us. Therefore, we acknowledge that a certain text may not mean what we think it means. We shouldn't use our interpretation of what God says in the Word to hold Him hostage to our expectations.

Reading with humility means you pray and ask the Holy Spirit to illuminate your understanding. Reading with humility means you place your heart in a teachable posture. No matter how smart or well-versed we are in the Scriptures, God is smarter than us! And on a practical level, reading with humility means not suffering through translations you don't understand. When I was growing up, my church read only the King James Version of the Bible. But if that version is too archaic and antiquated for you, there are so many other versions at your disposal that will help you to have a better understanding. Never be too proud to ask your spiritual leader for help in understanding the Scriptures. This is what it means to approach the text with humility.

We should also approach the Scriptures with honor. Reading Scripture with honor means never forgetting this is a sacred text. The Holy Scriptures are fundamentally about a holy God and His plan to save an unholy people from their sins. When we do not honor the sacred worth of this text, we treat God's Word like any other book. We consult it the same way we turn to a self-help book. This is not to say that God can't speak through the newspaper or from a journal or through a fictional character. God can reveal Himself in anything He created because all of creation testifies to His existence. But the Holy Bible is different than other texts. Second Timothy 3:16 says, "All Scripture is God-breathed and is useful for teaching, rebuking, correcting and training in righteousness." The Holy Spirit inspired the writers of this text to produce the manual for our lives. When we lose honor for the holiness of the Scriptures, something important gets lost. Jesus didn't worship the Scriptures, but He reverenced them. We should do the same.

Also, Scripture should be read with a hermeneutic of love. Each time you read it, you have to remember God loves you. Everything you read must be seen through this lens. If you had a strict guardian growing up, he or she may have made you feel circumspect and nervous when walking into a room. When they approached you, you may have hid because you thought they would speak forcefully or condescendingly to you. If they called your phone, you answered it thinking, "What did I do wrong?" Implanted in your psyche was the assumption that you were bad at your core, and therefore, anything your parent said, you heard it with an ear bent toward self-condemnation and disparagement.

How many of us approach the Scripture in that same way? We assume God is mad at us and wants to punish us. But this is the furthest thing from the truth. Reading the Bible with a hermeneutic of love means God ultimately wants you to win. His love is wide. His grace is deep. His justice is for your peace. His commandments are for your protection. He does what He does and He says what He says because He wants you to flourish. Whenever you read Scripture, see yourself as the apple of God's eye—because you are!

WORSHIP

The subject of worship is as broad and as wide as the Atlantic Ocean, but for the purposes of this chapter, I want to focus on it as a spiritual discipline because it is. Jesus modeled this in several ways, but I'd like to focus on two of them. He models worship as intentional engagement with God, and secondly, demonstrates that corporate worship is equally as important as private worship.

In John 4 we encounter a woman in Samaria who thinks she knows worship better than the God who created it. Jesus meets her at Jacob's well, and they embark on a conversation about the true nature of worship:

> The Samaritan woman said to him, "You are a Jew and I am a Samaritan woman. How can you ask me for a drink?" (For Jews do not associate with Samaritans.)
>
> Jesus answered her, "If you knew the gift of God and who it is that asks you for a drink, you would have asked him and he would have given you living water."

> "Sir," the woman said, "you have nothing to draw
> with and the well is deep. Where can you get this
> living water? Are you greater than our father Jacob,
> who gave us the well and drank from it himself, as
> did also his sons and his livestock?"
>
> Jesus answered, "Everyone who drinks this
> water will be thirsty again, but whoever drinks
> the water I give them will never thirst. Indeed, the
> water I give them will become in them a spring of
> water welling up to eternal life."
>
> —JOHN 4:9–14

As this woman speaks with Jesus, she tells Him where
the Jews worship and where people like her worship. But
Jesus explains that worship is not a place; it's a posture.
He reorients her understanding about worship because
He knows the location of your body is not more important
than the posture of your heart. Jesus knows what many
of us are still learning—namely, that it doesn't matter
where you are; if your heart is not postured toward God,
then you have missed the essence of worship.

Worship is a Christian imperative if we are aiming to
be like Christ. It's what Christ says the Father is seeking
in John 4. When we worship the Lord, we engage Him
with intention and reverence. When we worship the Lord,
we concentrate our lives on the Supreme Being. In an age
ripe with idolatry and a compulsive need to place people
on the altar of our hearts, where only Christ belongs,
worship must be a daily part of our lives. In prayer you
can be you. In worship you can forget about you.

When Jesus resists Satan's offer to bow down and
worship him, what He shows us is the heart of a true
worshipper. Worship is more than affection; it is the

acknowledgment of God's invaluable worth and a commitment to express that worth by placing Him above all else. Worship reveals where our allegiances lie. No one in a relationship wants affection without allegiance, and it's the same way with God. When you value someone, you demonstrate your valuation of them by committing to them both privately and publicly. Although this allegiance is the foundation of worship and the heart of a worshipper, I am not saying that we can reduce worship to privatized allegiance.

Private worship and public worship are equally important. Many are comfortable with and emphasize the significance of private worship. It's a beautiful and intimate space carved out for you and God. However, I am noticing a growing trend that deemphasizes the significance and necessity of public and collective worship. As a pastor, I often hear the claim, "I can worship at home," which is true and troubling at the same time. It's true in the sense that worship can be done in the privacy of one's own home. But if that line of thinking assumes that worshipping at home exempts one from the responsibility of collective worship with other believers, then that is troubling. I am aware that we live in an age when people can view church services online and worship in the comfort of their homes. And we praise God for the accessibility that technology affords! However, those avenues should be a supplement but not a substitute for the collective worship experience that the writer of Hebrews clearly says should not be forsaken (Heb. 10:25). Privatized Christianity isn't biblical Christianity. We are born into a spiritual family that we are to grow with, serve with, and worship with when we are able to do so. When we intentionally remove ourselves from these environments, we miss out on a beautiful encounter with God that can't happen in isolation.

Imagine if the people who gathered in the Upper Room during Pentecost decided to stay home. What would've happened or not happened if they said, "I can do this on my own"? There is something inexplicable about corporate worship that changes our perspectives and drives us closer to God. Jesus knew this, which is why He would frequent the temple. It's interesting—in one instance Jesus enters into the synagogue to turn over the tables (Matt. 21:12). He knew there was corruption going on in the temple, but He never stopped going! If Jesus did not use the imperfection of the synagogue as an excuse to abandon corporate worship, how can any of us use the imperfection of the church to do the same?

I am well aware that we may have to cease attending *a* church, but that should not cause us abandon *the* church. There may be times when we have to make adjustments, but we should not avoid corporate worship, because we really do need it. Corporate worship experiences bring us closer to God and closer to our community. I've experienced this reality countless times in my own life and witnessed it in the lives of others. I witnessed one particular incident with a young woman who wrestled with substance abuse. She struggled with the incessant use of alcohol and was addicted to heroin and crack cocaine. However, she attended a worship gathering at our church one night where we were engaging in an extended period of worship.

During our time of worship she sat down a bit perplexed. But while she sat there that night she had an encounter with God. She sensed His nearness, she discerned His comfort, and she experienced His power. As a result, she had what I commonly call an anointed anomaly. In other words, she experienced a miracle. She was miraculously set free from all her addictions and is now faithfully serving as a volunteer in our congregation. I am not in any way suggesting that every story ends the way hers did; however, this was her experience. The collective worship experience created a welcoming environment for God's presence that she was able to encounter because she was in the midst. She was the beneficiary of an environment that she couldn't create herself. This is one of the many benefits of the collective worship experience and one that God doesn't want any of us to miss out on.

SERVICE

Service is another activity not often seen as a spiritual discipline. But if we are to live like Christ, then service cannot be seen as an optional exercise. Service is a regular practice. It is not only something Christians do to give back to society; it is the heartbeat and pulse of our call to discipleship. Jesus modeled this on the very night that He was betrayed:

> After that, He poured water into a basin and began to wash the disciples' feet, and to wipe them with the towel with which He was girded. Then He came to Simon Peter. And Peter said to Him, "Lord, are You washing my feet?"
>
> Jesus answered and said to him, "What I am

doing you do not understand now, but you will
know after this."

Peter said to Him, "You shall never wash my
feet!"

Jesus answered him, "If I do not wash you, you
have no part with Me."

Simon Peter said to Him, "Lord, not my feet
only, but also my hands and my head!"

Jesus said to him, "He who is bathed needs only
to wash his feet, but is completely clean; and you
are clean, but not all of you." For He knew who
would betray Him; therefore He said, "You are not
all clean."

So when He had washed their feet, taken His
garments, and sat down again, He said to them,
"Do you know what I have done to you? You call Me
Teacher and Lord, and you say well, for so I am. If
I then, your Lord and Teacher, have washed your
feet, you also ought to wash one another's feet. For
I have given you an example, that you should do as
I have done to you."

—JOHN 13:5–15, NKJV

The beautiful imagery in this passage is a message in
itself. On the last meal Jesus was to partake in with His
disciples, He intentionally chose to wash their feet. It's
the last deed He did before He was arrested and perse-
cuted. If it is true that what someone does last is most
important, then washing the disciples' feet is a clue into
how important service was to Jesus. When Peter denied
Jesus the privilege of service, he missed the lesson Jesus
was trying to teach. The point of Jesus doing what He
did was to show the disciples what He expected them to

do as well. Jesus never asks us to do what He doesn't do Himself. He is not the kind of leader who expects to be served. Instead, He modeled the blessing of servanthood.

There is no way that we can accurately represent Jesus without emulating His commitment to serve others. Through His service, Jesus introduced a new modus operandi for the believer. I understand that I communicated in chapter 1 that love should be the brand of the believer, but service is one of the ways that love is expressed. As a matter of fact, the ultimate way that Christ demonstrated His love for us was through the sacrifice that He made by giving His life. He served us by sacrificing for us. Remember, Jesus says in Matthew 20:28, "Just as the Son of Man did not come to be served, but to serve, and to give his life as a ransom for many." Jesus instructs and admonishes His followers to follow in His footsteps.

We can carry out this commandment in a number of ways. We can and should serve our local churches by giving our time, treasure, and talents. We can serve by praying for coworkers, helping children with homework, or simply lending a helping hand to our neighbors. We can also serve by aiding and assisting the least of these and organizations that serve those in need. However, service is not just a way to *act like Jesus*. Serving actually helps *make us more like Jesus*. I contend that serving is just as spiritually formative as prayer, fasting, Scripture reading, and worship. In other words, serving helps you see if you are growing and helps foster growth.

Can you imagine the humility and love Jesus had to possess to stoop down and wash His disciples' feet? He washed Peter's feet, the one that would deny Him three times. He washed Thomas's feet, the one who would doubt the authenticity of His resurrection. This type of activity can't be accomplished by the immature. Serving is grown folks' business. The willingness to do so is an indication that one is maturing in spiritual virtues. It's easy to read a book on humility; it is much more difficult to actually live with humility. Service is a tool that God uses to teach us virtues that can't be learned from textbooks but only in the school of experience.

I have found this to be true in my own life and in the lives of others. One of the requirements for every ministry in our church is to engage in two outreach activities a year. Although as a church we engage in a number of initiatives locally and globally such as adopting underprivileged schools; cleaning up parks and playgrounds; serving the homeless by collecting clothes, food, and supporting community organizations; we also expect every member in our church—whether they work as greeters, on the parking team, or in media—to get outside the walls of our church twice a year and serve some aspect of the community. We understand that the community benefits from their service, but I realize that our members benefit more than those they serve.

I hear tons of testimonies about how serving has impacted people, helping them become more appreciative, more loving, and patient. However, one particular testimony sticks out to me the most. There was a gentleman from our church who was part of a ministry whose project was to distribute blankets to the homeless. While doing so he engaged in a conversation with a gentleman who happened to be homeless. That became the catalyst for an epiphany this church member would never forget. He assumed, unfortunately like many people, that this man was homeless because he was uneducated, unmotivated, and unwilling to receive assistance. Another way of putting it was this church member was being a bit judgmental. However, while conversing with this gentleman he discovered that the man possessed multiple graduate degrees but lost his wife and daughter in a tragic car accident, and consequently had some mental health challenges that led to his losing his employment and residence. The young man from our congregation shared this story with me with tears in his eyes because he was shaken by the fact that he was unknowingly judgmental of this people group until he actually served them. His experience in serving helped him become aware of a blind spot in his life, an area in which he needed to grow. Just like serving helped this young man have that eye-opening and growing experience, so it is a tool God can use to help us do the same.

THE FABULOUS FIVE WILL SHAPE YOU

After considering these five modes of discipline, I hope you are encouraged to strengthen your spiritual muscles that need exercise. The more you work these spiritual disciplines, the more they will work for you. To experience a life like Christ in public, you've got to do what He did in private. In order to be a disciple, you must be disciplined. It's as simple as that.

When Jesus tells His disciples to pray and not give up in Luke 18, He is encouraging them to make prayer a priority. When He says, "If you love Me, keep My commandments," He is challenging His listeners to study the Word so they can live out those commandments. When He says, "The hour has come and now is the time to worship," He's pushing us above the clouds and into another realm of glory so we can see life from heaven's perspective. When He says, "What you have done to the least of these, you have done to Me," He's calling us to serve others as if they are angels unaware. Finally, when Jesus says, "These things go out by fasting and prayer," He means what He says.

Jesus knows discipline will bring out a new level of power in your life, but most of His hearers in the Gospels do not experience that power. Why? Because it can only be unearthed when we move from hearing to doing. If you desire the power that comes through discipline, then I encourage you to internalize these benefits and challenge yourself to be in public what you have cultivated in private.

Chapter 8

JESUS and RELATIONSHIPS

In the beginning, God created you for relationships. He made you to relate to him and to others. Miss out on relationships, and you're missing the core reason for which God put you on this planet....A life without relationships may well be a simpler life, but it is also an empty life.[1]
—TOM HOLLADAY

ONE DAY, WHILE riding down the road, I had an interesting epiphany. A skunk was lying in the middle of the street. He had obviously been unsuccessful in his attempt to cross the road. As a result, I had to drive through a rather unpleasant odor. While doing so, I realized what I smelled was actually a defense mechanism. The liquid that secretes from skunks is an odor so foul it has been known to ward off animals as aggressive as bears. The odor is one way skunks defend themselves.

I then realized God created every creature with a defense mechanism. Cheetahs are extremely fast. Deer are extraordinarily agile. Scorpions sting, birds fly, and lions are strong. But what about us? What do we humans do to defend ourselves? We can't fly like a bird, and we can't run as fast as a cheetah, so how do we ward off aggressive attackers?

Then it came to me. Humans have something other species in the created order do not have. We have the gift of an amazing mind. It is an invaluable gift from God. We possess a thinking capacity that is absolutely unparalleled.

This gift should be stewarded gratefully and faithfully. The adage still rings true today: *A mind is a terrible thing to waste.* When we waste our minds and don't maximize our God-given capacity to think through life's pivotal turns, we lose our given mode of protection. We relinquish a crucial part of our humanity. When we don't work our minds, we "unemploy" our purpose.

In his book *Renovation of the Heart* Dallas Willard says that "the prospering of God's cause in the earth depends upon his people thinking well. We cannot pit good thinking against strong faith."[2] I'm nowhere near as articulate as Dallas Willard, so I'll just say what my father used to say: "Use your head!"

Christians in particular must be careful not to follow their hearts while failing to use their heads. It's not heart *or* head but heart *and* head. I'm simply saying we must be careful not to become so entangled in our emotions that we don't consider the weight of our decisions. Christ commanded that we love the Lord with our entire hearts, minds, and souls, but most of us overlook the mandate to love with our whole mind. The mind is the bridge that communicates what the heart wants and what the soul needs. When our minds are sharpened, our goals become clear. If our mind spotlights the wrong things, we will end up like that skunk in the middle of the road: helpless and incapacitated.

Mind Over Matter

If there is one area in which we must put this principle into practice, it is in the area of our relationships. Our greatest joy and greatest pain come from relationships. Weddings, births, and family reunions are catalysts for great joy, but divorce, funerals, and arguments cause some of our greatest pain. People are imperfect, trouble is inevitable, and life is a mixture of pleasure and pain. But some pain can be avoided if we utilize our minds, specifically in this area.

By and large, relationships tend to be the place where people lead with their hearts instead of their heads. If this is true in your life, then I'm sure it's also challenging for you to figure out how to relate to people. Oftentimes our emotional intelligence affects our relational intelligence, so if we live by how we feel and allow our emotions to dictate our interactions concerning who can enter or exit our lives, then we will certainly lose the value of the unique gift God gave for our protection—our minds. All of that to say this: failure to guard your emotions will result in a world of trouble.

Have you ever purchased an item because it excited your emotions, only to realize it didn't fit you as nicely as it did the mannequin? If your mind had had a conversation with your emotions before you purchased the outfit, you would've thought, "Let me try this on before I leave." But impulsive buyers spend quickly without considering the ramifications. Marketing managers know this, which is why they create ads a certain way to attract a certain demographic during certain peak seasons. Jesus knew this too, which is why He succeeded in living a balanced life with others—a model that we will closely consider for the remainder of this chapter.

But before we continue, please do not misunderstand my observation. Your emotions are gifts from God, and I'm not suggesting we should engage life without them. We just can't always believe our emotions. Emotions are tremendous translators of one's mood, feelings, and expressions—but when it comes to how we relate to others, our emotions can cloud our judgment. They can convince us to stay in a situation we desperately need to leave, or to leave a situation we need to stay in. Emotions are tentative and ephemeral. Today you may want companionship; tomorrow you may want breathing space. Today you may fear the hard conversation; tomorrow you may want to knock down someone's door to confront them. Today you may want to change your major based on a bad test grade; tomorrow you may meet the greatest mentor, who convinces you to stick it out. To sum up, we can't make decisions based purely on emotions. We need to let our minds—God's gift to us—play a role in what we do, especially when it comes to our relationships.

RELATIONSHIPS CHANGE US

Relationships are extremely consequential. They are catalysts for pleasure and pain. As a result, your greatest pleasure and greatest pain will often come from the same place: people.

Look at what the Scriptures teach about relational impact:

> Walk with the wise and become wise, for a companion of fools suffers harm.
>
> —PROVERBS 13:20

> As iron sharpens iron, so one person sharpens another.
>
> —PROVERBS 27:17

> Do not be misled: "Bad company corrupts good character."
>
> —1 CORINTHIANS 15:33

In three short verses we see the power in and the profundity of human relationships. According to Proverbs, you can get wisdom simply by walking with someone who is wise. If that isn't amazing, I don't know what is! The disciples became smarter just by hanging out with Jesus. But the opposite can happen if you entertain foolishness. Bad company corrupts good character. Therefore, some people become products of their poor environments even though they are genuinely nice people. Bad people are not always bad, but they can be bad for you. You have to use your mind to figure out which is which.

Don't you see? Relationships are extremely consequential. For this reason, we cannot afford to steward them with and by our emotions alone. An engaged mind is crucial. Please don't leave home without it!

A better word for the mental exercise required to stay fit in this life filled with relationships is *discernment*. Discernment is the ability to perceive an unspoken truth about something or someone. It goes beyond the mere appearance of a thing. You hear her words, for instance, but you see her heart. You hear his apology, but you know it isn't coming from a genuine place.

Being discerning doesn't mean being cynical, hyper-suspicious, or paranoid. It is not the same thing Paul speaks of when he discusses the discerning of spirits in 1 Corinthians 12:10. No, discernment is a virtue. Paranoia is a vice. Discerners catch what others overlook. In every relationship, you must learn how to discern. Read the fine print and see beyond the headline details.

Jesus taught His disciples to marry their emotions to discernment. He interacted with people from all walks of life every day of His life—but He used His mind, not just His heart. He interacted with paralytics in a different way than Pharisees. He connected with crowds one way but counseled His disciples in another way. If you want to do relationships better, follow the road map of Jesus Christ, for only He can teach you how to differentiate parasites from assignments and partners from promoters.

WHO'S AT YOUR TABLE?

Jesus models discernment in a very powerful way. There He is, enjoying the Last Supper with His disciples. As we've already seen in part, during this momentous occasion, Jesus washes the disciples' feet and talks to them about modeling Christlike behavior. Meanwhile, betrayal is brewing between the lines of a seemingly normal situation:

> The evening meal was in progress, and the devil had already prompted Judas, the son of Simon Iscariot, to betray Jesus. Jesus knew that the Father had put all things under his power, and that he had

come from God and was returning to God; so he got up from the meal, took off his outer clothing, and wrapped a towel around his waist. After that, he poured water into a basin and began to wash his disciples' feet, drying them with the towel that was wrapped around him.

He came to Simon Peter, who said to him, "Lord, are you going to wash my feet?"

Jesus replied, "You do not realize now what I am doing, but later you will understand."

"No," said Peter, "you shall never wash my feet."

Jesus answered, "Unless I wash you, you have no part with me."

"Then, Lord," Simon Peter replied, "not just my feet but my hands and my head as well!"

Jesus answered, "Those who have had a bath need only to wash their feet; their whole body is clean. And you are clean, though not every one of you." For he knew who was going to betray him, and that was why he said not every one was clean.

When he had finished washing their feet, he put on his clothes and returned to his place. "Do you understand what I have done for you?" he asked them. "You call me 'Teacher' and 'Lord,' and rightly so, for that is what I am. Now that I, your Lord and Teacher, have washed your feet, you also should wash one another's feet. I have set you an example that you should do as I have done for you. Very truly I tell you, no servant is greater than his master, nor is a messenger greater than the one who sent him. Now that you know these things, you will be blessed if you do them.

"I am not referring to all of you; I know those I have chosen. But this is to fulfill this passage of

Scripture: 'He who shared my bread has turned against me.'

"I am telling you now before it happens, so that when it does happen you will believe that I am who I am. Very truly I tell you, whoever accepts anyone I send accepts me; and whoever accepts me accepts the one who sent me."

After he had said this, Jesus was troubled in spirit and testified, "Very truly I tell you, one of you is going to betray me."

His disciples stared at one another, at a loss to know which of them he meant. One of them, the disciple whom Jesus loved, was reclining next to him. Simon Peter motioned to this disciple and said, "Ask him which one he means."

Leaning back against Jesus, he asked him, "Lord, who is it?"

Jesus answered, "It is the one to whom I will give this piece of bread when I have dipped it in the dish." Then, dipping the piece of bread, he gave it to Judas, the son of Simon Iscariot. As soon as Judas took the bread, Satan entered into him.

So Jesus told him, "What you are about to do, do quickly." But no one at the meal understood why Jesus said this to him. Since Judas had charge of the money, some thought Jesus was telling him to buy what was needed for the festival, or to give something to the poor. As soon as Judas had taken the bread, he went out. And it was night.

—JOHN 13:2–30

I'd like for you to notice two things here: what Jesus does and what He doesn't do. Jesus serves His disciples. He does not budge. He knows every person at the table.

He speaks to Peter and insists on washing His feet. He addresses Judas by saying in no uncertain terms, "Do it quickly." In one scene and in just a few short interchanges, Jesus answers the question, "How do we treat unlikable people?" No matter who they are or what their motives are, *Jesus remains exactly the same.* He doesn't change His personality to accommodate the flatterer or to assuage the fool. He blesses His enemies, and He blesses His friends. Jesus has utter confidence in Himself, for He "knew that the Father had put all things under His power."

This is a relationship model for the ages. When you live in the fullness of your Christlike identity, talkative Peters and traitor Judases will never again intimidate you. When you live in the fullness of your Christlike identity, you will be able to stand confidently in who you are. You will carry out your assignment with ease because you have finally accepted what Jesus demonstrates here—namely, people do not own your peace.

Jesus does not perseverate over Judas. He is neither worried nor frantic. He never begs Judas to change his mind because His discernment can read the fine print. When we beg betrayers, we give them power. When we plead for supporters, we lose our power. If someone is bold enough to betray you, then nothing you do right now will change their heart. Be yourself, regardless. The Christlike response would be to say to them what Jesus said to Judas: "Do it quickly."

Your betrayer cannot control your destiny. God is in control of your life. Whatever your betrayer attempts to do will not destroy who you are. If anything, it will only prepare you for the impending promotion that suffering for the name of Christ guarantees.

When we do not cater to Judas, our response honors God. Our reaction demonstrates the utmost confidence we have in Jesus and not in the relationships in which we find ourselves. Judas's actions did not determine the final word over Jesus's life. Jesus knew that. In the same way, people do not own your story! God is the author and finisher of your faith. Therefore, if people try to put you in the grave, the Father will raise you up. If your mother and father forsake you, the Lord will take you above it. The power belongs to God. The only way relationships can gain more power over you than God is if you give that power away.

The overall lesson here is to know who is at your table. Know who is there to serve. Know who is there to be served. Know who is there to assist. Know who is there to learn. Know who is there to teach. Use discernment.

When you know someone, you study his or her behaviors onstage and offstage. You pay attention to their tendencies, proclivities, and patterns. We all have patterns—whether good or bad—and our patterns reveal the core of our character. Who we are is wrapped up in what we continually do. Jesus had discernment as sharp as a two-edged sword because He spent time with His disciples. He knew their patterns. He knew before Peter spoke out of turn that he would speak out of turn. Why? Because Peter always spoke out of turn! It's impossible to have a thriving relationship with a person with whom you have not spent significant time.

Depending on where people sit at your table, that should determine how much time you allocate to them. Just accept it and move on. Everyone will not occupy the same place in your life.

Several years ago I taught a message titled "Put People in Their Place." The message was motivated by the way I saw Jesus managing His relationships with the disciples. He had what some biblical historians call the "inner circle," which consisted of three disciples: Peter, James, and John. These three were with Jesus on the Mount of Transfiguration and at the Garden of Gethsemane. They saw Him in times of strength and in moments of weakness. In the same way, people who are in our inner circles should be people we can trust when we are at our best and when we are at our worst. I noticed that Jesus never apologized to the other nine disciples for not giving them the access to Him the other three had. He understood that everyone has a place and everyone cannot carry out the same role. This is not a "respecter of persons" scenario. It just means you understand the importance of having healthy boundaries in relationships.

Just like Jesus knew who was at His table, we should know who is at the table of our lives and place them accordingly. Everyone should be treated right, but not everyone should be treated the same. A married person does not treat their boss the same way they treat their spouse, even though Christlike love is required in both contexts. In the same way, Jesus had an inner circle of friends whom He called upon during difficult times: Peter, James, and John. He loved every disciple equally, but He selected three to be closer than others. We must do the same.

Know who is who in your life. Align your relationships according to a pattern, and accept that everyone will not be your best friend. You cannot align a relationship if you do not define that relationship. How did Jesus define relationships? That's what we're going to talk about next. He did it through a process I like to call "fruit inspection."

Fruit Inspection

> Watch out for false prophets. They come to you in sheep's clothing, but inwardly they are ferocious wolves. By their fruit you will recognize them. Do people pick grapes from thornbushes, or figs from thistles? Likewise, every good tree bears good fruit, but a bad tree bears bad fruit. A good tree cannot bear bad fruit, and a bad tree cannot bear good fruit. Every tree that does not bear good fruit is cut down and thrown into the fire. Thus, by their fruit you will recognize them.
> —Matthew 7:15–20

If we are not careful, we will easily become judgmental and condescending after reading passages such as this. It's a great passage about relationships, but it must be read with a Christocentric hermeneutic. (Remember when we talked about that? It means reading through the lens of Christ.)

Each verse in this chapter provides a practical way to take inventory of our relationships without judging an individual. The first verse begins, "Do not judge, or you too will be judged." Here, Jesus is not suggesting we police every person who walks into our lives. It is impossible to do that. Instead, He wants us to pay attention to people's actions. We have to make assessments that include what we see and hear, not just how we feel.

In order to know a tree by its fruit, we must see the exterior of the tree and acknowledge the outside layers for what they are while paying attention to its interior. This is what it means to discern. If we do not cultivate relationships from the inside out, then we could have a Judas at our table but not know the difference between his words of flattery and John's consistent love. Not knowing the difference between these two can be a setup for a letdown in our relationships.

Jesus advises that we cut down any tree that does not bear fruit after a year. What do I mean when I say bear fruit? Well, fruit serves a number of purposes, one of which is to be a source of nourishment that ultimately strengthens us. A fruitful relationship is one that in some way or another nourishes us. Just as fruit provides our body with nutrients it needs, a fruitful relationship provides our life with things it needs. One of my good friends is an associate pastor at the time of this writing and also a comedian. One of the ways he nourishes my life is through his ability to lighten my mood. Whenever I speak with him, he always makes me laugh. I don't think it is intentional; he is naturally comedic, and he nourishes me with laughter. The nature of my work can be stressful at times, and laughter is something my life needs. My relationship with him is a fruitful one because it provides me with what I need as opposed to what I don't. Every relationship won't nourish us the same way, but a fruitful one nourishes us nonetheless. It adds value to your life. You may not always be able to immediately identify how it nourishes you, but you will know that it nourishes you. Pause for a moment and think about your relationships. Are they good fruit?

Now, with that in mind, along with Jesus's admonition to cut down any tree that doesn't bear fruit for a year, consider: How many years have you been tolerating a toxic relationship? It may be time to cut it down in order to save your life. If you have ever worked at a company or dated a person who drained the life out of you, then you know what it feels like to experience the pain of a misplaced relationship. Not only do you suffer, but also your true friendships and genuine supporters—those whose attention you should've been focusing on instead of catering to this fake friendship—suffer as well. Every investment made into a bankrupt relationship will affect the potential interest of future relationships. You can't deposit the same check at two different banks. Your deposit has already been made elsewhere.

When we know those who labor with us, we inspect our relationships like fruit. We look at every dimension of the relationship. We use all of our senses to evaluate the truth. When we don't ask important questions or overlook obvious habits, we end up in a mirage relationship. People who need to be closer become further away, and people who need to be far away gain access to the esoteric details of our lives. Just accept it: certain relationships have to be managed and honored differently. This is the point of Matthew 7. Do not judge—but inspect!

FOUR KINDS OF RELATIONSHIPS

I can hear you saying it already: "Dharius, I understand what you're saying, but how do I do that? How do I discern and define who is who in my life?" Here are four categories I hope will offer some insight on how to define and align some of your relationships. The people in our lives can be categorized as parasites, assignments, partners, or promoters.

Parasites

Parasites are biological organisms that live and are sustained at the expense of the host. They release waste and toxins into the body of the host, and they feed off the host and offer no adequate or useful return.

There are many symptoms to having a parasite, but let's explore just a few here that relate to our purposes. First, sleeping disorders are common when you have a parasite. During the night, your body normally works to eliminate toxins via the liver. Parasitic infections interrupt this process and upset the rhythm of the body. In the end, they make it impossible for you to rest. Parasitic relationships are the same way. They make it impossible for us to rest. No, I'm not talking about your children, your spouse, or your parents. I'm talking about those other relationships that consistently make withdrawals without making deposits. If all a relationship is doing is causing you restlessness, then it may be a parasitic relationship.

Teeth grinding is another symptom of having a parasite. A parasitic infection causes a condition known as bruxism, or abnormal grinding, clenching, and gnashing of one's teeth. While parasitic relationships may not cause us to grind our teeth—well, maybe they will!—they will definitely cause us to grind in life. When a parasite relationship exists in your life, you have to work harder than you usually do in order to accommodate them. If all the relationship does is make everything harder, it may be a parasite.

Thirdly, parasites cause dysfunctions in the immune system. Oftentimes, when you have a parasite living inside of you, it will leech vital nutrients from the body, forcing the immune system to operate with a poor supply of vitamins, minerals, and energy sources and leaving a person more vulnerable to attack. In a similar way, if a person makes you spiritually, emotionally, and financially weak, they may be a parasite—and parasites are hazardous to your health.

After hearing this description of parasitic relationships you may have come to the conclusion that you are in one (or two or three). If that is the case I would like to offer some guidance on what to do. First of all, understand that you have a responsibility to be a good steward over your life. If something or someone who is a part of your life jeopardizes your health and progress, then you must address it. I say this because when I reflect on my personal and pastoral experience, I have discovered that there is often glue that keeps people stuck to parasitic relationships, and that glue is guilt. We tend to feel a sense of obligation and indebtedness to people who have been a part of our lives for a significant period of time. Therefore, when it comes time to shift and/or sever the relationship we can feel as if we are "abandoning" them. However, you must realize that some relationships are seasonal and the other person's well-being is ultimately God's responsibility and their own.

The second way to deal with parasitic relationships is to take responsibility for change that needs to be made. It is unwise and unrealistic to wait for someone else to get the revelation that his or her behavior is harming you. You will find yourself frustrated and extremely agitated if you attempt to do so. You must realize that your life is your responsibility, and when others can't see that what is happening isn't good for you then you must see it and take action.

Thirdly, sever the relationship completely or shift it so that their dysfunction no longer depletes you. I mention these two options because sometimes the parasitic relationship is with someone you can't avoid for the rest of your life. It could be a sibling, coworker, or parent. In those cases, when you can't avoid interaction, you should set boundaries that determine what you will and won't subject yourself to, and then act accordingly. This is shifting the relationship. For example, shifting the relationship doesn't necessarily mean you don't talk to the person; it may mean you don't talk to him as much or that you limit your conversation to certain content.

Finally, to deal with a parasitic relationship, learn to be OK with the fact that the other person in the problem relationship may not be OK with the changes you seek. In my own life, I have often found myself hoping and wishing that others would be OK with decisions I had to make that were in my best interest. There were times when people understood why I had to make certain choices and there were times when they did not. In either case, I couldn't allow my concern for their opinion to cause me to renege on promises I made to myself about me. Jesus didn't. He often made decisions that those around Him didn't agree with. Peter didn't agree with Him going to the cross. However, Jesus didn't allow his opinion to stop Him from doing what was in line with His destiny. Neither can you. Your destiny awaits. Your purpose is calling. People are in need, but you won't have anything to give to those who want what God has placed within you if you waste those gifts, talents, and resources on those who don't appreciate it and are really just concerned about themselves.

Assignments

Parasites should not be confused with assignments. Assignments are ministry connections. They are different than parasitic people because while they may take from you and be needy in some ways, God has assigned them to your life for a particular purpose. Your job is to do your part and help your assignment. Render service to them as a service to the Lord.

You'll likely find that assignments don't reciprocate, but that's OK. They may also think they love you, but what they actually love may be your gift, and that's OK too. God put you in their life to help them. That's what you're there for.

On that note, here's a word of caution: Do not date your assignment. Do not marry your assignment. Love that person enough to help them accomplish their purpose, and look for no earthly reward from the person you are called to assist. God is going to reward you for your labor because God puts assignments in your life for a purpose.

Partners

Partners are purposed in your life to build you. They are willing to walk alongside you without being intimidated by you. They bring gifts and talents to the table that aid and assist you, and you do the same for them. Their joy comes from seeing you become a greater version of yourself.

Partners are resourceful people. They may not bring an equal amount of resources to the table, but they definitely bring something. Paul and Silas were partners in the ministry. When Paul was in prison, Silas sang and prayed with him. His presence was enough. He was not as popular as Paul, but he was nevertheless significant to the work they were doing. Together they were able to spread the gospel and save even the prison guard who imprisoned them.

When discerning your partners, look for loyalty and affirmation. Partners tell you the truth, but they do so in love. They are not "yes men" or "yes women," but they also do not complicate the simple things. They are the first people you think to call when you have an idea. They add excitement to your life and offer helpful advice when you can't see a blind spot. Partners give life. They never take life away. Through thick and thin, they will be with you. When you need someone to talk to in the middle of the night, they are there and will pick up the phone.

Promoters

Promoters help you access or attain that which you do not have the ability to attain yourself. Samuel was an important prophet in the Old Testament who promoted David to kingship. Elizabeth was crucial to Mary's birthing process. Her experience helped Mary to carry the Son of God within her womb. Promoters are mentors, teachers, coaches, and managers. They've either been where you are going or they know how to bridge the gap between carrying a desire and reaching your destiny. These relationships are important, as God uses them to get you to the place He has for you, so be sure to honor them.

JESUS KNEW THEM ALL

Jesus experienced the reality of all these types of relationships. He had to manage parasites, assignments, promoters, and partners. The Sadducees and Pharisees were at times parasites to Jesus. They were righteous in their own eyes, but they sucked the spiritual life out of people. The disciples were partners to Jesus because they had access to Jesus in a way others did not. They saw Him sleep, eat, and pray. They saw His public miracles but also wrote about His private grief. Jesus's assignments were those who received miracles from Him, such as the blind man in John 9 or the lepers at the gate. His assignments received assistance from Him, but they weren't expected to follow Him. Not everyone you help will partner with you. But the good news is, you don't have to expect them to. When assignments leave, promoters will come. John the Baptist was one of many promoters Jesus had. He promoted the kingdom of God everywhere he went. He knew he was called to set the stage in preparation for Christ, and he did just that.

Know this: parasites, assignments, partners, and promoters will show up at your door. Your job is to know whom to dismiss at the door, whom to help in the living room, and whom to invite to the table. The better we become at identifying the promoter, the parasite, the assignment, and the partners in our lives, the better we will be able to manage our relationships as Jesus did.

Chapter 9

JESUS and WORDS

Sticks and stones may break our bones,
but words will break our hearts.[1]
—ROBERT FULGHUM

EVERYONE READING THIS book is guilty of carrying a concealed weapon. Yes, even you. And no, I am not referring to a canister of eye-burning Mace, nor am I referring to a razor-sharp pocketknife. I am alluding to a weapon that is sharper than any knife and burns much more than Mace. It is a ubiquitous weapon among us. This weapon is our tongue. As you have the power to talk, you are armed and dangerous.

Many of us have heard it said, "Sticks and stones may break my bones but words will never hurt me." But all of us who have lived beyond age two know this is not true. I agree with Robert Fulghum, who has revised that statement to say, "Sticks and stones may break our bones, but words will break our hearts."

The reality is, words hurt. Words pierce. Words poison. If a teacher tells a student she isn't smart enough, those words can have long-lasting consequences. One student will apply to Harvard anyway. Another student may drop out of school tomorrow. When a doctor tells a patient they have only a few months to live, immediately the body begins to react around those words. Isn't it interesting how words on a screen or a voice on a message can ruin or improve your entire day? You hear the phone ring and decide not to answer, not knowing it was the last conversation you would have with a loved one. She doesn't leave a message, and all you can think now is, "If only I could've heard her voice one last time."

Our words shape our culture. Our words reveal our character. Based on certain words, I can guess your profession or passion because we tend to speak in the language of what we love. It's a dangerous thing to assume God can change our hearts and our minds but not our words. It's a harmful thing to speak quickly and hear slowly. But many of us shoot a host of innocent bystanders every day with our words because we have not yet learned how to tame our tongues.

Proverbs says, "The tongue has the power of life and death, and those who love it will eat its fruit" (Prov. 18:21). The fruit of your words will help or hurt, elevate or subjugate, liberate or imprison. But let's go a little deeper. Sometimes your words are good but your tone needs training. Has anyone ever said to you, "It's not what you said but how you said it"? Or maybe, "What you said was right, but the timing was wrong"? When we speak about the weapon of the tongue, I don't want you to think about the use of words only. Also think about the tone, the timing, and the temperature of your words. Most arguments graduate from anger to hatred or disagreement to violence because of these three elements of tone, timing, and temperature. If your words are sizzling hot, this may not be the best time to release them. If your words are said after someone has suffered immense loss, then don't be surprised if what you say yields an unfavorable reaction. The tongue is pregnant with the potential to give birth to life, vitality, hope, and peace. It's all about how we choose to use the weapon.

Dr. Martin Luther King Jr. used his words to build people up and bring peace. He never picked up a weapon to fight. Instead, he let his words swing for him. His philosophy was one of nonviolent direct action, which means he talked people out of the depravity of segregation. Others were convinced the world would only change through militant force and retaliation. But Dr. King adopted another way. His words sparked change in racial, social, and economic policies during the civil rights movement.

Words, like money, are amoral. Depending on the user, words can build you or break you. The same way Scripture was used in the past to humiliate slaves and degrade women, Scripture can be used to liberate the disenfranchised and eradicate gender bias. It's all in the way you use and understand the power of your words.

By the end of this chapter I pray you will think about the side effects of a seemingly trivial conversation. I hope the way Jesus uses His words will motivate you to turn your weapon of mass destruction into a powerful tool of motivation. I desire that we all ask ourselves "How would Jesus speak about this?" instead of rushing to give someone a piece of our mind. If we are going to accurately and appropriately re-present Jesus, then this is an area we must manage well.

The Weight of Words

Jesus is the ultimate example of someone who managed His tongue well. He modeled for us how to manage our words in a way that honors God and helps others. Unfortunately, though, a lot of damage has been done to the image and effectiveness of Christianity because of irresponsible verbosity. Some people are absolutely incapable of or unwilling to manage their tongues, and this produces a kind of death in the public's perception of Christians. Throughout this entire chapter, remember: you hold life and death in your tongue.

The tongue can build people up or it can be an instrument that accomplishes evil, provides problems, and tears people down. Some of the greatest pain inflicted on individual lives has come from the concealed weapon of the tongue. One biblical writer says it is "a small part of the body, but it makes great boasts. Consider what a great forest is set on fire by a small spark. The tongue also is a fire, a world of evil among the parts of the body. It corrupts the whole person, sets the whole course of one's life on fire, and is itself set on fire by hell" (James 3:5–6).

Jesus knew the power of words in such a way that He practiced thoughtful communication in one situation and responded silently in another. He asked rhetorical questions in order to expose ulterior motives, and He modeled what it means to be quick to hear and slow to speak. Quite simply, Jesus just knew what to say, when to say it, and how to say it. Matthew 12 proves it. As you read each verse, notice how words influence the outcome of this narrative:

Then they brought him a demon-possessed man who was blind and mute, and Jesus healed him, so that he could both talk and see. All the people were astonished and said, "Could this be the Son of David?"

But when the Pharisees heard this, they said, "It is only by Beelzebul, the prince of demons, that this fellow drives out demons."

Jesus knew their thoughts and said to them, "Every kingdom divided against itself will be ruined, and every city or household divided against itself will not stand. If Satan drives out Satan, he is divided against himself. How then can his kingdom stand? And if I drive out demons by Beelzebul, by whom do your people drive them out? So then, they will be your judges. But if it is by the Spirit of God that I drive out demons, then the kingdom of God has come upon you.

"Or again, how can anyone enter a strong man's house and carry off his possessions unless he first ties up the strong man? Then he can plunder his house. "Whoever is not with me is against me, and whoever does not gather with me scatters. And so I tell you, every kind of sin and slander can be forgiven, but blasphemy against the Spirit will not be forgiven. Anyone who speaks a word against the Son of Man will be forgiven, but anyone who speaks against the Holy Spirit will not be forgiven, either in this age or in the age to come.

"Make a tree good and its fruit will be good, or make a tree bad and its fruit will be bad, for a tree is recognized by its fruit. You brood of vipers, how can you who are evil say anything good? For the mouth speaks what the heart is full of. A good man brings good things out of the good stored up in him, and an evil man brings evil things out of the evil stored up in him. But I tell you that everyone will have to give account on the day of judgment for every empty word they have spoken. For by your words you will be acquitted, and by your words you will be condemned."

—MATTHEW 12:22–37

Matthew 12 begins by sharing important information with us, telling us the man brought to Jesus is blind and mute. To some this was not a unique situation because Jesus had healed many blind people before. But not many of them were blind *and* mute. To be mute means he could not speak. To be blind means he could not see.

Whether you realize it or not, all of us were blind and mute before someone brought us to Jesus. We had physical sight but no spiritual vision. We were talking a lot but communicating very little. This passage shows us the power of encountering Jesus. When Jesus touches you and you come into relationship with Him, one of the first things He does is enable you to see and speak differently.

What good would sight be if your tongue refused to change? When Jesus comes into our lives, our eyes open. We see things in a new way. The world looks different. Scriptures read differently. We see circumstances differently. And this new insight trickles into how we live. All of a sudden, we can rejoice during moments when others would cry. All of a sudden, our judgmental lens is replaced with a redemptive hope. Everyone we see has the potential to be better. We no longer see them as sinners in the hands of an angry God but as children in the arms of a loving Father. Your sight affects your insight. And once your insight changes, your communication changes as well.

Once Jesus healed the man in Matthew 12, he was no longer mute. Therefore, he could tell others what it was like to be blind. In like fashion, when Jesus opens your eyes, it's impossible for you to remain silent. Speaking about Christ is a reflexive and automatic reaction to encountering Him.

But let me flip this observation on its head. If you are carriers of that same light, do people receive sight from you? As a Christian witness, does God use your words to open others' eyes? Or are your words the very prisons that lock people up? How do people see you when you leave their presence? Even better, what components of their vision and conversation change because they encountered you? These are the hard questions we must answer in order to better gauge the implications of our words. When we look like Christ, people should not leave our presence without scales falling off their eyes.

Perhaps many of us can take a lesson from this story. Not only did Jesus heal the man's eyes, but He also healed his mouth. Is it possible God needs to heal your tongue? Have you become so negative in your perception that you only speak in pessimistic terms? Maybe your mouth needs a healing—for when your mouth gets healed, you may find more opportunities to be quiet and still. When your mouth is healed, you won't run to the phone to gossip; you will run to your knees to pray. When your mouth is healed, you will catch yourself speaking and living like Jesus.

As the text continues to unfold, we bump into people

whose mouths have not been healed. But the good news is we can learn from their mistakes and live by Jesus's example. Three of the most transformative lessons in this text are as follows: Jesus spoke good, not gossip; Jesus gave joy, not judgment; and Jesus told them who they could be, not who they used to be.

SPEAK GOOD, NOT GOSSIP

Our words should be instruments for good and not receptacles for gossip. The Pharisees in Matthew 12 misidentified Jesus as a demon. Instead of keeping their thoughts to themselves, they spread false truths amongst the community. This is gossip at its worst. Any form of idle, unproductive conversation about the affairs of another is gossip. It doesn't matter if we heard it from a cousin of a friend of a coworker; it is information at best and a rumor at worst. When we spread it around or allow others to spread it to us, it becomes gossip.

In Romans 1:29 Paul includes the pettiness of gossip among its evil and divisive cousins—strife, deceit, and envy. As followers of Jesus, gossip should never be a part of our makeup. I'm so glad Jesus isn't a gossiper. He is our High Priest. He is the one who knows our innermost thoughts and secrets. I think we all would be in big trouble if Jesus were irresponsible with His tongue. We shouldn't be either. Our mouths should speak good and not gossip.

The Pharisees didn't do this, but I love how Jesus deals with them. He asks them to think about their accusation that He is Satan. If that were true, He would be dividing Himself against Himself because He is casting Himself out. I love it! Instead of arguing with them, He points out the illogical nature of their argument. He reveals how unintelligent their gossip was, and consequently, how unintelligent gossip always is. It is unintelligent because it doesn't just hurt the person being talked about; it also hurts the person doing the talking. Gossip is a trust thief. It robs you of the right to be trusted. God can use people who aren't perfect, but it's hard for God to use those He can't trust. Jesus revealed that the Pharisees couldn't be trusted.

Jesus also rose above the pettiness of their conversation, and Christians who speak like Jesus rise above the conflict and chaos around them. We turn rumors into opportunities for repentance. We turn gossip into another way to see the gospel. We do not sit idly by and allow other people to be disparaged. Instead, we speak up and present the good in the midst of the gossip.

There is one addiction that it's OK to have, and it's an encouragement addiction. The Book of Hebrews advises us to "encourage one another daily...so that none of you may be hardened by sin's deceitfulness" (Heb. 3:13). If you watch Jesus, you see that He was addicted to encouraging people. "Rise, take up your bed and walk" (John 5:8, NKJV). "Your faith has made you well" (Mark 5:34, NKJV). "This day you will be with Me in Paradise" (Luke 23:43, NKJV). These are all amazing examples of the encouraging words of Jesus. Even when He lovingly rebuked people, He modeled encouragement. And in Matthew 12 Jesus encourages His negative accusers to think about their actions. He educates them on matters of the kingdom, and He frees them from the assumption that their actions are OK. We should do the same.

GIVE JOY, NOT JUDGMENT

Our words are opportunities for joyful affirmation, not judgmental condescension. If we follow the advice of Paul and let our conversation be "as it becometh the gospel of Christ" (Phil. 1:27, KJV), then we would speak less and pray more. The kingdom of God is righteousness, peace, and joy in the Holy Ghost (Rom. 14:17, KJV), so our words should reflect the kingdom we represent. Every text message and e-mail we send should be righteous, peaceful, and joyful. When we use these three words as a rubric for communication, I believe our conversations will become much shorter. Who we speak to on a daily basis might change. Most importantly, people will remember that we are called to be witnesses, not the judge.

Judgmental communication assumes we are God when we are not. The Pharisees judged the situation happening in Matthew 12. Instead of recognizing the healing power of Jesus Christ, they attributed the miracle to an evil spirit. They said it was the work of the enemy. Their error teaches us the importance of bridling our tongues. Matthew 7:1–5 and Romans 2:1 are two helpful guideposts to remember when we find ourselves judging others:

> Do not judge, or you too will be judged. For in the same way you judge others, you will be judged, and with the measure you use, it will be measured to you.
>
> Why do you look at the speck of sawdust in your brother's eye and pay no attention to the plank in your own eye? How can you say to your brother, "Let me take the speck out of your eye," when all

the time there is a plank in your own eye? You hypocrite, first take the plank out of your own eye, and then you will see clearly to remove the speck from your brother's eye.

—MATTHEW 7:1–5

You, therefore, have no excuse, you who pass judgment on someone else, for at whatever point you judge another, you are condemning yourself, because you who pass judgment do the same things.

—ROMANS 2:1

The Pharisees in the Matthew 12 text did the exact opposite. Not only did they judge Jesus, but also their judgment was inaccurate! Very often, people judge what they don't understand. How many times has someone accused you of something prematurely? What is sad is that because the Pharisees didn't have all of the necessary information, they were irresponsible in their judgment and committed blasphemy by slandering the Spirit of God. Our lesson from the Pharisees is simple: judge not, no matter what! When you step into a situation you don't fully understand, pray about it. Don't talk about it.

Jesus is antithetical to the Pharisees. Throughout the Gospels we hear Him using words to bring joy and not judgment. In John 15, for instance, Jesus self-identifies as the true vine and identifies His Father as the gardener. Verse by verse He explains the purpose of the branches, the interconnectedness of love, and the importance of abiding and remaining in that love. He explains the purpose of this lecture in John 15:11: "I have told you this so that my joy may be in you and that your joy may be complete." Jesus was a promoter of joy, not judgment.

In order to sound like Christ, then, our words also should be wrapped with the residue of joy. So let's pause for a moment and ask a question: How do people feel when they leave your presence? I'm not saying we're to be in the "feel good" business, but I am encouraging us to honestly audit our lives to determine whether or not our words bring people joy or cast judgment.

TELL THEM WHO THEY CAN BE

Our words should also point people forward, not backward. The most effective way to communicate is to tell others who they can be, not to remind them of who they used to be.

Interestingly this kind of prophetic forward-pointing is littered throughout the entire Bible. When God changes someone's name, He is pointing to who they can be. He changed Abram's name to Abraham, Sarai to Sarah, and Jacob to Israel. The new name given represents their new purpose and destiny. Jacob's name meant "trickster," and his life was filled with deceitful moments. But when he wrestled with the angel, his name was changed to Israel. His new name represented his new status.

This is what Christians should emulate when we communicate with people. Never bury people in the valley of past mistakes. Instead, build them up. Encourage them to focus on who they are going to become.

Jesus does this with Simon Peter, and the implications are absolutely profound:

Andrew, Simon Peter's brother, was one of the two who heard what John had said and who had followed Jesus. The first thing Andrew did was to find his brother Simon and tell him, "We have found the Messiah" (that is, the Christ). And he brought him to Jesus.

Jesus looked at him and said, "You are Simon son of John. You will be called Cephas" (which, when translated, is Peter).

—JOHN 1:40–42

When Jesus changes Simon's name to Cephas, He is telling Simon who he had been was not the only indicator of who he would be. I am not saying that one's past does not impact his future; I'm saying his past doesn't determine his future. I believe this is one of the reasons Jesus changed Peter's name. The word *Cephas*, which is translated *Peter*, means "rock." Every time Peter heard his name called, he heard rock! Come here, Rock! Pick this up, Rock! I'm praying for you, Rock! The name change isn't necessarily about how others saw Peter but about how Peter saw himself. Jesus wanted Peter to see himself differently. He wanted him to see who he could be and who he would be.

The change of a name denotes a change in character, and even a change in direction. When people encounter us, the goal is that they walk away better. Remind them of who they can be and not what they used to be. Even if you know their past, don't imprison them in it.

When we talk like Jesus, we are always pointing forward. We are always speaking life. This doesn't mean we avoid confrontation, but when we do confront a problem, we speak life into it in such a way that it produces a solution.

THE WORDS ARE THE ROOT

By the end of the narrative in Matthew 12 Jesus explains that our words can justify us or condemn us. He never says our *actions* will justify us or condemn us because it's our words that are the bedrock of everything we do. If our tongues are like fruit, then the quality of our tree will reveal itself in what we say and how we say it. The mirror of our words will reflect the content of our heart, and if we are like Jesus, then we will sound like Him.

Remember, Jesus spoke good, not gossip; Jesus gave joy, not judgment; and Jesus told people who they could be, not who they used to be. After a twenty-four-hour day, have your words matched this template? Where do you need to grow the most? How do you speak about yourself to others? If what we say about ourselves is negative and judgmental, then outsiders will have no choice but to be affected by the toxicity inside of us.

My prayer is that you will watch your words and shape them after Jesus. May Psalm 19:14 be your prayer today and always: "Let the words of my mouth, and the meditation of my heart, be acceptable in thy sight, O Lord, my strength, and my redeemer" (KJV).

Chapter 10

JESUS and FORGIVENESS

*Forgiveness is the economy of the heart...for-
giveness saves the expense of anger, the
cost of hatred, the waste of spirits.*[1]
—HANNAH MORE

H E CHEATED ON you. You thought he was loyal.
You thought he was your knight in shining
armor. You never expected your marriage to
end like this. But the divorce papers have been served.
You are rebuilding life from the ground up. And you were
actually doing all right until you drove past a billboard
that read, "Forgive him."

She left you for someone else. Without warning, you
came home and she was gone. The pain is so immense,
you can't eat. You can't sleep. Now you have to manage
life without her. Was she ever your soul mate to begin
with? Did she really love you? You open the Bible hoping
to find a scripture that will give you permission to retal-
iate, but Jesus's words leap from the pages: "Forgive sev-
enty times seven."

You've never known your biological parents. You feel

alone. They abandoned you, so you perpetuate the trauma of unresolved pain in every relationship you encounter. At work, you sabotage new friendships because your trust has been bruised. You don't enjoy life—you're just coping. Five minutes into your first therapy session, the counselor asks the one question you've never answered: "Whom haven't you forgiven?"

It kills you on the inside. You shouldn't have done it. You saw the warning signs. You knew today's pleasure would yield tomorrow's pain, but you still did it. You still pursued it. You still gave in. And now you can't seem to forgive yourself.

Forgiveness is a tough cookie to bite into. In fact, when you really get down to the core of human hurt, you will always find an area reserved for unforgiveness. It's the sting that keeps on stinging and the hurt that keeps on hurting. It enters in through an insensitive word, a selfish act, or an unintentional deed, but whenever it comes, it's sure to stay for a while.

As Christians, we can't give unforgiveness a permanent key to the door of our hearts. It can visit, but eventually it has to go. Jesus commands us to admit it, confront it, and then forgive it. The hardest part is to forgive it, but everything we do, even the hard stuff, is for God's glory and for our good. When we obey, our response brings God glory. Not only that, but it also yields good harvest for us in return. When we fail to obey and when we resolve to do things on our own time and with our own process, it interferes with God's glory and sentences us to a self-induced prison.

As hard as this chapter may be for some to read and ingest, it is necessary and essential. If we are going to really re-present Jesus, we must learn the art of forgiveness.

Jesus is the ultimate example of one who walks in forgiveness. In the final moments of His earthly life He asks God to forgive the very people who were performing His execution. In Luke 23:34 Jesus said, "'Father, forgive them, for they do not know what they are doing.' And they divided up his clothes by casting lots."

What makes Jesus's prayer of forgiveness so powerful is the mere fact that the people He forgave didn't even ask for it—and at that point weren't even sorry. Are you sure you want to be like Jesus? Are you still committed to re-presenting the Jesus of the Bible? If so, it means following His example and following His instruction to walk in forgiveness. However, in order to do so, we must be clear on what forgiveness is and—more importantly— what it isn't.

LET'S START WITH THE PRELIMINARIES

Like every other term covered in this book, a concept of forgiveness lives in our minds, and a concept of forgiveness lives in the Scriptures. Our overarching goal is to make sure the definition in our heads is consistent with the way Jesus saw this subject. How did Jesus deal with forgiveness? What did He say? To answer these questions, let's first investigate what forgiveness is not:

1. *Forgiveness is not forgetting or pretending it didn't happen.* What happened has happened, and you will not wake up one day devoid of memory. Forgiveness is about

learning the lesson without holding on to the pain.

2. *Forgiveness is not excusing unbiblical and unhealthy behavior.* It does not mean accepting what happened as appropriate or permissible. If you have been injured and done an injustice, you have a right to be upset about it. But forgiveness is about deciding, "I'm not going to allow another person's wrong to rob me of my joy."

3. *Forgiveness is not the issuing of a license for someone to repeat the behavior.* Just because you forgive someone does not mean you have to live the same way you lived before the incident occurred. Sometimes even after forgiving someone you have to reposition yourself so that you don't continue to experience the perpetuation of that activity.

4. *Forgiveness is not restoration.* Hopefully every relationship will achieve some level of reconciliation, but forgiving a person doesn't mean the relationship will automatically be restored to the same state. Trust is critical to any relationship. In order for the relationship to exist in your life, trust must be earned.

Knowing what forgiveness is not helps us determine what forgiveness really is. In the words of T. D. Jakes, forgiveness is "letting it go."[2] Letting what go? Resentment, bitterness, the desire for revenge, and indignation.

Forgiveness is an act and expression of grace. Like grace, it is unearned. Like grace, it's something we don't deserve. An unknown sage once said, "Forgiveness is me giving up my right to hurt you for hurting me."

In his book, *The Peacemaking Pastor*, Alfred Poirier says you will find two types of forgiveness: transactional and unilateral.[3] *Transactional forgiveness* is when someone requests forgiveness and it is granted. In order for this kind of forgiveness to work, two separate parties must comply—the one asking for forgiveness and the one granting it. Once a request is made and the recipient agrees, a transaction is made. Whether the end result is "I forgive you" or "I'll think about it," someone has requested forgiveness and someone else has granted or denied the request.

Unilateral forgiveness is when the offender does not request forgiveness but we grant it anyway. Jesus forgives unilaterally in Luke 23:34 when He says, "Father, forgive them, for they do not know what they are doing." If we only read these verses during Easter presentations, we may miss the revelation of this moment. As I mentioned earlier, Jesus is asking God to forgive people who aren't even sorry—people who never say "I messed up" and who are still, in fact, persecuting Him. In the midst of blatant wrongdoings, Jesus unilaterally forgives them.

In the same way, there are times when we must forgive those who have done us wrong, whether they apologize or not. Don't hold your heart hostage waiting for someone to apologize to you. Some people are too ignorant to apologize, some are too arrogant to apologize, and some are too embarrassed to apologize. If you wait for them to come to their senses, you will never be free.

You have the key to unlock the shackles from your own heart. The key is forgiveness.

HOW HAVE YOU BEEN FORGIVEN?

Matthew 18 records an amazing story where Jesus emphasizes the significance and importance of forgiveness:

> Then Peter came to Jesus and asked, "Lord, how many times shall I forgive my brother or sister who sins against me? Up to seven times?"
>
> Jesus answered, "I tell you, not seven times, but seventy-seven times.
>
> "Therefore, the kingdom of heaven is like a king who wanted to settle accounts with his servants. As he began the settlement, a man who owed him ten thousand bags of gold was brought to him. Since he was not able to pay, the master ordered that he and his wife and his children and all that he had be sold to repay the debt.
>
> "At this the servant fell on his knees before him. 'Be patient with me,' he begged, 'and I will pay back everything.' The servant's master took pity on him, canceled the debt and let him go.
>
> "But when that servant went out, he found one of his fellow servants who owed him a hundred silver coins. He grabbed him and began to choke him. 'Pay back what you owe me!' he demanded.
>
> "His fellow servant fell to his knees and begged him, 'Be patient with me, and I will pay it back.'
>
> "But he refused. Instead, he went off and had the man thrown into prison until he could pay the debt. When the other servants saw what had happened, they were outraged and went and told their master everything that had happened.

"Then the master called the servant in. 'You wicked servant,' he said, 'I canceled all that debt of yours because you begged me to. Shouldn't you have had mercy on your fellow servant just as I had on you?' In anger his master handed him over to the jailers to be tortured, until he should pay back all he owed.

"This is how my heavenly Father will treat each of you unless you forgive your brother or sister from your heart."

—MATTHEW 18:21–35

When Peter asks Jesus about forgiveness, Peter doesn't pick the number seven arbitrarily. Rabbinic commentaries suggest that a person should forgive three times, so Peter was actually attempting to be generous when he said seven times.

But Jesus's answer was far greater than Peter's generosity could imagine. Jesus said we are to forgive seventy-seven times, which was another way of saying forgiveness has no limit. Forgiveness has neither an expiration date nor a statute of limitations. A follower of Jesus should remember the countless times God has forgiven him or her, and in response, reciprocate to others.

I know this concept is difficult to grasp. Jesus anticipated it would be, and this is why He unpacked the concept of unforgiveness through a parable. He begins, "This is the way the kingdom works," and then He paints a picture of a king, a servant, and a fellow servant. The king is God, of course, and we are recipients of the gracious forgiveness God gives us. But what the forgiven servant does to his fellow servant is a portrait of what we often do to others. Back then, ten thousand bags of gold was the equivalent of millions of dollars. A hundred silver coins was drastically less in value than what the servant owed the king. But instead of forgiving his fellow servant, the forgiven servant develops emotional amnesia. He forgets what the king has done for him. He forgets that his debt was canceled and decides not to forgive someone else who owes much less.

The same is true for us. In comparison to the sins for which the King has forgiven us, we have no justified reason to refuse forgiveness to others. We cannot hold someone else hostage for a hundred denarii when we have been forgiven ten thousand. Remember, you were forgiven for the debt others knew about as well as the debt God covered. You were forgiven for the things that almost ruined your life, destroyed your family, and tore apart your relationships. When we evaluate the truth of our lives and calculate the sum total of our experiences and downfalls, I'm sure we all can admit how ridiculous it would be to withhold forgiveness from someone else.

Jesus uses this parable to help His listeners examine themselves, and we are meant to examine ourselves as well. Has the King given you a gift you are withholding from someone else? Have you become so focused on your losses that you've ignored the exponential gain? Do you recognize that unforgiveness only yields spoiled fruit in your life? Would it be so hard to settle the account, cancel the debt, and let the person go? When you free them, you free you. So, forgive.

WHO IS THE OTHER SERVANT?

Another aspect in this text is worth considering. Clearly, the king is God. Clearly, we are the servant who receives forgiveness. But who is the other servant? Who are the ones we don't forgive, and how can we learn to extend forgiveness to people we don't necessarily like? To answer these questions, I want you to imagine that the other servant is another person, God, or yourself.

Other people

If the servant represents others in your life, this person may be, for some, a father, an absent relative, or a significant other. This person's absence may speak louder than their presence, but still Jesus commands us to forgive them. Why? Because sometimes their absence is a blessing in disguise. Sometimes absence produces in you the determination to be better and not bitter. Sometimes absence helps you to empathize with those like you. Sometimes absence gives you the courage to speak to the silent tears in someone else's life.

Or maybe the other servant in this story is an ex who ruined your life or a relationship that destroyed your focus. You can't seem to get over the fact that you gave that person years of your time, and no matter how much you try to forgive them, you can't redeem what was lost. You're aware of how much of your life you missed, and there's nothing worse than doing a lot and accomplishing nothing.

No matter the context or the story, Jesus commands us to forgive. It is what Jesus had to do when Judas betrayed Him, when Peter denied Him, when Thomas doubted Him, and when others left Him. We should do the same. Whether the other servant is a former pastor, father or mother, sibling or coworker, you must release yourself from resentment. Forgive them so your heart can have the space it needs to breathe. Pray this prayer below as a way to get started:

Father, I am well aware that You know the hurt, the pain, and the disappointment I have lived with as a result of what was done to me. As a matter of fact, You not only know it, You also felt and feel it. I am having a hard time letting it go, and I need Your help. I realize that I need to forgive them more than they need my forgiveness. Help me to free my soul from the chains of unforgiveness. You forgave people who didn't deserve it and didn't ask for it, and I am asking You to help me to do the same. I repent for holding on to it as long as I have. You have forgiven me, and I have no right to withhold forgiveness from others. So by Your grace and through Your power, I am releasing it all to You and extending my forgiveness and grace. I am ready to be happy, ready to be whole, and ready to be healed. I pray that I am no longer paralyzed by the pain of my past. I let it go so that it can let me go. In Jesus's name, amen!

God

The fellow servant can also represent God for some of us. Yep, I said it. As difficult as it may be to confess, there are times when each of us will get upset with God—we're often just too afraid to admit it. Jonah was upset with God. David was upset with God. Moses was upset with God. And I suspect that someone reading this book is also upset with God. You had hopes and dreams. You had goals in mind to accomplish. You expected God to keep your loved one alive. You believed God for the miraculous to happen, and nothing changed. You're more than disappointed and more than angry. It has now metastasized into an infection called unforgiveness. Your Job-like season resulted in a different reaction. Job may have blessed the Lord in spite of the loss, but you want to curse God and die. Just admit it. God can handle your truth.

When the tidal waves of life produce a decline in assets, health, and relationships, we don't always respond like Christ. We often feel like the writer in Psalm 22:1, and we ask, "My God, my God, why have you forsaken me? Why are you so far from saving me, so far from the words of my groaning?" The logic of this disappointed psalmist is so similar to those moments when I have found myself disappointed by God. The psalmist assumes that if God is with him, God should have acted in accordance to his expectation. In other words, if God isn't doing what I want, then that must mean He isn't with me—that must mean He has forsaken me.

But there are too many examples to count the times in which God was present with someone in the Bible but did not do what they expected Him to do. Perhaps your perspective about the situation needs adjustment. What if God didn't forsake you but instead delayed His arrival like He did with Lazarus? What if God didn't speak to you like He did with Joseph so the journey itself could testify to the presence of God for you? What if God extended your life so He could bless your barrenness and give you what you laughed about, like Sarah did, years after the time you thought it would happen? When we are in the brunt of a test, the teacher never speaks. It doesn't mean he has left the classroom; it could just mean he's silently watching you pass.

If this is the case with your unforgiveness, then forgive God for the misconception you've brought into all of your life. God is present even when is seems He is not active. God is with you even when you can't feel Him. God is there even when you are not! When God moves and when God chooses to remain still, we must trust that whatever God is doing is in the best interest of His kingdom. This is why Jesus declared, "Not my will, but thine, be done" (Luke 22:42, KJV). Pray the prayer below:

> *Father, I love You with all my heart. However, I confess that there are times when I don't understand You and don't trust You as I should. At times I feel like I know what's best for my life, and that arrogance impacts the way I feel toward You. However, I realize that Your ways aren't my ways. You see things I don't see, You know things I don't know, and You are up to some things that are bigger than me. Forgive me for the resentment I have held in my heart toward You. Please give me grace to trust You even when I don't understand You. Give me the blessed assurance of knowing that You do all things well! In Jesus's name, amen!*

Ourselves

The final individual this servant can potentially represent is *us*. Yes, the final person you have to forgive is yourself. Forgiving yourself is about no longer holding yourself hostage to the person you used to be. You shouldn't hold yourself captive to a past you can't change.

Jeremiah prophesied about a day when God would say, "For I will forgive their wickedness and will remember their sins no more" (Jer. 31:34). If God can forgive it and forget it, so can you. If God can decide to un-remember, so can you.

Forgiving yourself doesn't change your past, but it will most certainly change your future. Paul says in Philippians 3:10–14:

> I want to know Christ—yes, to know the power of his resurrection and participation in his sufferings, becoming like him in his death, and so, somehow, attaining to the resurrection from the dead.
>
> Not that I have already obtained all this, or have already arrived at my goal, but I press on to take hold of that for which Christ Jesus took hold of me. Brothers and sisters, I do not consider myself yet to have taken hold of it. But one thing I do: Forgetting what is behind and straining toward what is ahead, I press on toward the goal to win the prize for which God has called me heavenward in Christ Jesus.

Remember, forgiveness is not acting as if it never happened, but determining not to allow what happened to steal your joy. It is deciding not to bury yourself in a grave that no longer fits the new creature you've become. It is the decision not to condemn yourself and chain yourself to past mistakes, because Romans 8:1 reminds us that there is no condemnation to those who walk after the Spirit. You have to forgive yourself, and then maybe you'll realize how easy it is to forgive others.

When we do not forgive ourselves, we imprison our

lives and incarcerate our hearts. Lewis Smedes says, "To forgive is to set a prisoner free and discover that the prisoner was you."[4] According to the parable in Matthew 18, Jesus says the one who could not forgive ended up in prison. The one who could not forgive ended up having to pay back debt to the king who had once expunged his charges. I wonder what would happen if you released yourself from the prison of unforgiveness. I wonder how much life would come back to you if you accepted a life without painful iteration of your past. I wonder how your health would change and how your relationships would flourish if you allowed God to vacuum the one place in your heart that has collected dust and cobwebs.

Each of us has that one place in our hearts or that one person who still pulls at our patience. We have that one person whose name we ignore when we see it on the caller ID. All of us have that one family member who frustrates us to no end. But underneath the frustration is a cemetery filled with regret, sadness, and bitterness. Sadly, however, the remains in that cemetery do not belong to the one we haven't forgiven; the remains belong to us. They are reminders of the place where our faith died. They are pillars of memories and traumas and dark moments that have taken control of our destiny and are trying to steal the little life we have left.

I charge you not to let it happen. Don't let unforgiveness destroy your freedom. Unforgiveness is not punishing the perpetrator; it's punishing you. It's putting yourself behind bars. But today, with the help of Christ, you will get free. Free to live like, love like, and look like Jesus.

Pray this prayer with me:

Father, I understand that there is nothing to gain by holding myself in unforgiveness and there is everything to gain by releasing myself from unforgiveness and beginning the process of healing. I want to move forward and make a positive difference in the future. I confess the ungodly accountability, self-abasement, and vows I have made to never forgive myself. Because Jesus died for my sins, I choose to forgive myself—to no longer punish myself and be angry with myself. I forgive myself for letting this hurt control me and for hurting others out of my hurt. I repent of this behavior and my attitude. I ask for Your forgiveness and healing. God, help me to never again retain unforgiveness in my heart. Thank You for loving me. Thank You for the grace to move forward with You. In Jesus's name, amen.

Chapter 11

JESUS and FAITH

To one who has faith, no explanation is necessary.
To one without faith, no explanation is possible.[1]
—St. Thomas Aquinas

IN 1986 BRITISH illustrator Martin Handford was asked to create an eccentric character that could be recognized in any crowd. After much deliberation, Handford concocted a time travel aficionado and world traveler. The cartoon figure dressed in the same getup every time we saw him: red and white stripes, a bobble hat, and a circular pair of glasses.[2] Out of what seemed like an arbitrary task came a series of children's books and international fame. The character's brand and image later expanded to a TV series, a comic strip, and video games promoting one famous question: "Where's Wally?" In North America the name Wally is translated Waldo. So in the Unites States we ask, "Where's Waldo?" But the concept of Waldo is the same. Each book challenges readers to find Waldo in the midst of a hectic crowd. At first it seems like an easy task. After all, his outfit is so unique. But the more clever and the more complex the illustration, the more difficult it is to find the real McCoy.

As we continue to compare the Jesus in our heads to the Jesus we find in the Bible, I can't help but draw a similarity between Waldo in the crowd and faith in the church. On the surface it would seem easy to find faith in a place where God is popular—meaning, the church—but the scarier truth is that not everyone who comes to church actually believes in Christ. Not everyone who claims to be a person of faith has placed his or her faith in God. This is why Jesus takes multiple opportunities in Scripture to describe faith. His objective is to help His disciples find God in the midst of a busy crowd.

Living like Jesus means living by faith, and walking with Jesus means walking by faith. Jesus's entire life was a life of faith. As a matter of fact, His willingness to die on the cross was not just an expression of His love for us; it was also a demonstration of His faith in the Father. Jesus was completely convinced the Father would raise Him back up again. He preached about it, He prophesied it, and He proved it. Faith is what motivated Jesus, and it is also what moves Jesus. The cross was a faith cross, and the tomb was a faith tomb. His life was an amazing example of what it means to have faith in our heavenly Father.

Therefore, if we are going to represent and re-present Jesus, then those of us who follow Him must be people of faith as well. However, in order to do so, we need to ask and answer a question: What kind of faith did Jesus have?

FAITH MATTERS

Journey with me through the Scriptures for a moment. I want to prove to you that faith is absolutely and unquestionably the gift Jesus responded to the most. Understanding this point will build a foundation for everything else in this chapter. So let's begin.

In Mark 5:34 Jesus tells a woman who had an issue of blood for twelve years, "Daughter, your faith has healed you. Go in peace and be freed from your suffering." Jesus is attributing her healing to the faith she had, not just to the power He possessed.

In Mark 10 Jesus encounters a blind man named Bartimaeus who needed a miracle. Jesus looks at him and says, "Your faith has healed you" (v. 52). Immediately the man receives his sight and follows Jesus along the road. Again we see how faith has the power to begin what Jesus's pronouncement solidifies.

In Matthew 9 Jesus encounters two blind men who approach Him with four humble words: "Have mercy on us." Jesus responds by challenging their faith: "Do you believe that I am able to do this?" They say, "Yes, Lord" and their yes grants them healing. Jesus concludes, "According to your faith let it be done to you; and their sight was restored" (vv. 27–30).

At least two or three dozen more stories like these exist in the Gospels. Certainly faith plays a crucial role to the ministry and life of Jesus Christ!

When reading these accounts of miracles, many readers tend to attribute the miraculous situations to Jesus alone—to His miracle-working power—but Jesus is constantly connecting miracles with faith. This isn't to suggest faith is more powerful than Jesus, but it does reveal how important faith is in the overall outcome of life.

Jesus responds to our faith. His power is most clearly seen when believers declare, "Lord, I believe." In the same way, when we don't believe, the Scriptures show us how that unbelief can stifle miracles as well. In Matthew 13, for example, Jesus returns to His hometown of Nazareth. While there, people only perceive Him as a carpenter's son. In other words, they keep relegating Him to their first encounter of Him. He's all grown up, but they keep reminding Jesus of when He was just a little lad, running around Nazareth with His parents.

I'm not sure what it is about certain people, but whenever you succeed or grow, they seem to find the utmost pleasure in reminding you of a time when you weren't so great. That's what they are doing to Jesus. They are bringing up His past in order to ignore His present. As a result, Scripture says, "And he did not do many miracles there because of their lack of faith" (Matt. 13:58).

When you look at faith through the eyes of Scripture and miracles being performed or not performed, it becomes even clearer: Jesus is looking for faith like children are looking for Waldo. So the question we now must consider and answer is this: If God stopped by our house today, would He find what He was looking for? Would He find a clever look-alike, or would He find the kind of faith Jesus responded to?

HAS YOUR FAITH WITHERED?

Faith is so essential to our Christian nature that the Bible says without it, it is impossible to please God (Heb.

11:6). I don't know any Christians who will boldly admit, "I want to displease God," but I know many Christians who have bought into a notion of faith that is not consistent with what Jesus teaches about it. As a result, we end up shooting an arrow with zeal but no knowledge. We end up missing the mark not because we didn't have a real desire, but because we lacked direction.

I want to help you reimagine faith in a fresh way. So let's look at Mark 11, where we find an interesting series of events that teach us what faith is and what faith is not:

> The next day as they were leaving Bethany, Jesus was hungry. Seeing in the distance a fig tree in leaf, he went to find out if it had any fruit. When he reached it, he found nothing but leaves, because it was not the season for figs. Then he said to the tree, "May no one ever eat fruit from you again." And his disciples heard him say it.
>
> On reaching Jerusalem, Jesus entered the temple courts and began driving out those who were buying and selling there. He overturned the tables of the money changers and the benches of those selling doves, and would not allow anyone to carry merchandise through the temple courts. And as he taught them, he said, "Is it not written: 'My house will be called a house of prayer for all nations'? But you have made it 'a den of robbers.'"
>
> The chief priests and the teachers of the law heard this and began looking for a way to kill him, for they feared him, because the whole crowd was amazed at his teaching.

When evening came, Jesus and his disciples went out of the city.

In the morning, as they went along, they saw the fig tree withered from the roots. Peter remembered and said to Jesus, "Rabbi, look! The fig tree you cursed has withered!"

"Have faith in God," Jesus answered. "Truly I tell you, if anyone says to this mountain, 'Go, throw yourself into the sea,' and does not doubt in their heart but believes that what they say will happen, it will be done for them. Therefore I tell you, whatever you ask for in prayer, believe that you have received it, and it will be yours.

—MARK 11:12–24

The background story here is too important to overlook, so allow me to "paint the crowd around Waldo" so you can see the masterful genius of our Messiah. Jesus has just ridden into Jerusalem for Passover. But it's late when He gets there, so He decides to stay in Bethany overnight. The next day He heads back to Jerusalem and gets a little hungry. There are no twenty-four-hour convenience stores in His day, so He has to find a tree with fruit on it for a morning snack. He sees a fig tree in bloom and goes for the fruit. When He gets close, He sees nothing but leaves. So He speaks to the tree and says, "May no one ever eat fruit from you again."

This tree is quite significant because throughout Jesus's ministry, trees were used as metaphors for people. Jesus said in one situation that you will know a tree by the fruit it bears (Matt. 7:17–20), and quite obviously, He was talking about people. In another situation He said, "I am the vine; you are the branches" (John 15:5). There again He was talking about people. So keep in mind that Jesus cursing the fig tree here in Mark 11 is a metaphor for people—which could possibly include religious people. Well, let me rephrase that—it probably *is* about religious people.

Nonetheless, what if Jesus is using this tree as an opportunity to talk about the church's withering faith? What if Jesus is using this tree to talk about the stifled faith in you and in me? After all, Jesus is hungry for food just like people are hungry for the Word of God. Jesus goes to a place that is supposed to be able to sustain Him, but when He gets close to it, it has no fruit. Just leaves. Just ornamentation. Most certainly the tree looks good from a distance, but upon further inspection, you realize it's useless if it is fruitless.

Jesus gets closer to the tree and realizes something else. The tree had an issue that time couldn't fix. Studies reveal Jesus approached the tree in April.[3] Figs were expected around May, yet figs were already on the tree! Jesus could tell, based on the season, this tree wouldn't have fruit the next month or the month after that. The tree had a deficiency that would continue to deceive people if it stayed there. No fruit meant no life, so Jesus cursed the tree. He cursed the tree to ensure it didn't deceive others. He wanted it to wither so people wouldn't keep running there to get fed and leave with unmet expectations.

But remember this is not about a tree. This is representative of a withering people. This is a metaphor about religious communities and our need to be cut down if ever we deceive people into believing our anemic tree has an abundance of fruit.

Jesus is clearly frustrated with Israel (the church during Jesus's time), so it makes sense why, in the middle of the tree scenario, the writer shifts to a scene in which Jesus is cleaning out the wickedness in the temple. The temple, you see, was like the fig tree. Jesus didn't have an issue with the system of sacrifice or the money itself. Remember how we learned money is amoral? Rather, His issue was the thievery and the trickery happening in the church. The system was a noble idea, but leaders began to pervert it and exploit people by overcharging them to change their money. The leaders had no concern for the lives of those they robbed. So Jesus starts cutting down trees, figuratively speaking. He runs people out of the temple and turns over the tables of money.

The text ensues. Evening comes and Jesus goes out of the city. Again they see that fig tree, but now it has withered. Remembering what Jesus said to the tree, Peter says, "Rabbi, look! The fig tree you cursed has withered." And Jesus says, "Have faith in God." Such an unexpected response, but when we put it all into context, we see the big picture. This encounter with the tree wasn't just about the tree; it was also about the disciples. Notice that Jesus did not simply say, "Have faith." He said, "Have faith in God." The encounter with the tree was an experience Jesus used to educate His disciples not just on the power of faith but also on the power of God. Your faith is only as strong as what or whom you put it in.

TELLING THE TRUTH ABOUT GOD

When Jesus speaks about faith, what does He mean? And when we say *faith* and Jesus says *faith*, are we talking about the same thing? When the Pharisees spoke of faith, they connected faith to keeping and observing the law. Their goal was to obey the Torah as if their lives were scientific experiments. When enlightenment teachers speak of faith, they speak in terms of optimism and hope and flowery beds of ease. But faith should not be confused with optimism. People can be optimistic and not necessarily have faith.

So, what does Jesus mean by faith? I heard someone once say: "Faith is acting like God is telling the truth!" It is rooted in the revelation of truth. Therefore faith's job is to get God what He wants for us, not always what we want for ourselves. I know that previous statement is problematic and troublesome for many, but I feel very strongly that it is true. Faith is not a weapon that can be used to hold God hostage to what we want. Faith doesn't create God's will; it achieves God's will. Our will and God's will are not always the same, and faith does not change that. Faith is acting like God is telling the truth, not necessarily that we are.

Telling the truth about what? First, about our salvation, which is saving faith; and second, about our specific situations, which is specific faith.

Saving faith pertains to our salvation. At the core of our Christianity is the understanding that we could never earn God's love. Ephesians 2:8–9 confirms, "It is by grace you have been saved, *through faith*—and this is not from yourselves, it is the gift of God—not by works, so that no one can boast" (emphasis added). Salvation isn't just given because of grace. It is also given because of faith—our faith. Our faith must trust that grace is enough to reconcile us to God. Our faith must trust that a thirty-three-year-old Jewish man's death on a cross and subsequent resurrection from a grave is all that is needed to resurrect a life.

However, faith in one area does not necessarily translate into faith in another. Someone can believe in the existence of God and God's ability to save but have trouble believing in God's ability to resurrect dead situations. The ability to believe God for specific situations is what I'm calling *specific faith*.

Often when people who desired divine intervention would approach Jesus during His time on the earth, He would ask a question, such as, "Do you believe I'm able to do this?" He wanted to know if they had faith for what they were asking for specifically.

When faith is specific, it looks a lot like what happened in Acts 14:8–10:

> In Lystra there sat a man crippled in his feet who was lame. He had been that way from birth and had never walked. He listened to Paul as he was speaking. Paul looked directly at him, saw that he had faith to be healed and called out, "Stand up on your feet!" At that, the man jumped up and began to walk.

The crippled man had a specific need. The man never said a word, but Paul discerned the specificity of his issue and healed him on the spot.

It's possible to have faith to be saved but not faith to be changed. This is exactly what Paul had to address in his letter to the churches in Galatia. In Galatians 3, he spends great energy and effort trying to get that church to see they had placed faith in Christ to start the transformative work in their lives but had started trusting in themselves to complete it. They had faith Christ could save them but not sanctify them. Another example can be found when Jesus visits His hometown of Nazareth in Matthew 13 and is greeted with skepticism and familiarity. Many asked the question, "Isn't this a carpenter's son?" Sadly, Matthew tells us that He did not do many miracles there because of their lack of faith. (Matt. 13:58).

Jesus couldn't do many miracles in Nazareth because of the people's unbelief. All the people saw was a carpenter's son, so that is all they got. What you see is what you get. If all we see when we look at Jesus is one who saves our souls, that is all we will get. But if we see and believe Him as the one who revolutionizes and changes every area of our lives, that's what we get instead—a God who has the power to move and change our lives in the here and now.

Faith Fertilizers

Because all faith is not the same, it's important to move on from the basics. In other words, many of us have only satisfied ourselves with saving faith and nothing more. But this kind of settled thinking reminds me of the Israelites who could believe God to deliver them from Egypt but never entered into Canaan.

In what areas of your life have you settled for basic faith? Where is God challenging you to believe Him in ways Jesus can respond to? We all know what it's like to mentally struggle with faith when it comes to certain areas, whether it's our children, job, marriage, health, or ministry. When faith is absent in these areas, worry and anxiety crop up.

Faith, like anything else, must grow and be developed.

I want to share four faith fertilizers that I believe will help develop a Jesus kind of faith in us.

Faith Fertilizer #1: Intimacy with God

Intimacy with God doesn't just happen. It requires intentionality. It's hard to believe in someone you don't know, and the better you get to know someone, the easier it is to believe them. Faith works the same way. Faith can only be as strong as the credibility and reliability of the person in whom you have faith. So if you don't know someone's credibility or if they continue to falter on their promises, then it's difficult to have faith in them.

Jesus, however, was positively convinced and secure in His relationship with the Father. This kind of confidence contributed to His faith during challenging situations like what happened in John 11, when Jesus raised Lazarus from the dead:

> So they took away the stone. Then Jesus looked up and said, "Father, I thank you that you have heard me. I knew that you always hear me, but I said this for the benefit of the people standing here, that they may believe that you sent me."
>
> When he had said this, Jesus called in a loud voice, "Lazarus, come out!" The dead man came out, his hands and feet wrapped with strips of linen, and a cloth around his face.
>
> Jesus said to them, "Take off the grave clothes and let him go."
>
> —JOHN 11:41–44

Can't you hear the intimacy in those words? "Thank you for hearing me. I knew that you always hear me."

Jesus has ultimate faith in the Father. Embedded in this verse is a bond that is not easily broken. Confidence like this comes through the cultivation of intimacy, in and out of season.

Intimacy is for sale. Yes, I meant what I said—intimacy is for sale. However, you can't buy it with money. The currency for intimacy isn't dollars and cents. It's time. If you want to experience intimacy with God—or anyone, for that matter—you must be willing to pay the price of time. By that, I mean daily, consistent, uninterrupted time through worship, prayer, and the study of the Word.

It's true in real life too. My wife and I have a dedicated date night because we realize there's no neutral gear in our relationship. Every relationship is either going forward or backward, never stalled in one place. In the same way, there's no neutral zone with God. We are either growing hotter or colder; He doesn't do lukewarm.

If we were to follow Jesus throughout the Gospels, you would see a man who craved to be with the Father. Time after time, He would leave His disciples and commune with His heavenly Father. I believe one of the reasons He was able to trust God so firmly was because He knew God so intimately.

Faith Fertilizer #2: Information from the Word

Not only does our faith grow through intimacy with God but also through information from the Word. In order for anything to grow, it must be fed. God's Word is like faith food. It feeds our faith with the information we learn, believe, and grow from. The more we learn, the more stock we place in our faith account.

Without this discipline of learning from the Word, our

lives will be plagued by two problems: unbelief or misbelief. Unbelief is simply the inability or unwillingness
to believe God's promises as revealed in God's Word.
Misbelief, on the other hand, is often overlooked but
equally dangerous because it's about believing the wrong
things. It happens when an individual builds his or her
life on untrue information. But God's Word is not God's
Word when it isn't accurately interpreted.

In my role as pastor I often have to communicate messages to people through others. From time to time the
message that's delivered isn't the message I gave. That
doesn't mean someone intentionally misrepresented me.
It just means someone didn't accurately interpret what I
said, and as a result, delivered a message that wasn't consistent with my intention.

Just as this happens from time to time with me, it
happens on a much grander scale with God. Some messages people deliver don't represent Him because they
were misinterpreted. When someone believes this, they
are misbelieving and begin to have expectations of God
that are not supported by Scripture. This leads to frustration, disappointment, and in extreme cases, abandoning
the faith. I call this spiritual food poisoning.

This is why Paul always instructed those he mentored
to pursue doctrinal accuracy—because misinformation
causes misbelief. Learning the Word helps provide us
with information that we can believe, and it also cor-
rects misinformation we've previously received so we can
believe God accurately. Paul says:

> How, then, can they call on the one they have not
> believed in? And how can they believe in the one

of whom they have not heard? And how can they hear without someone preaching to them? And how can anyone preach unless they are sent? As it is written: "How beautiful are the feet of those who bring good news!"

But not all the Israelites accepted the good news. For Isaiah says, "Lord, who has believed our message?" Consequently, faith comes from hearing the message, and the message is heard through the word about Christ.

—ROMANS 10:14–17

In order to cultivate faith (especially when you want to grow in specific faith), you must discipline yourself to read and listen to the Word. Faith comes by hearing, which is why God calls, anoints, and sends teachers into our lives to help us understand the Scriptures. Both reading and listening are imperative to our faith being strengthened.

Remember, when we read the Scriptures, we feed our faith. When we do not read the Scriptures, we starve it.

Faith Fertilizer #3: Healthy environments

Have you ever heard someone say, "You are what you hang around" or "Birds of a feather flock together"? Both of these phrases point to the importance and influence of our environment. It is extraordinarily difficult to cultivate great faith if you are surrounded by unbelief. This is why Jesus in one instance puts out the noisy and unbelieving crowd before He is able to perform a miracle (Matt. 9:23–25).

In the same way, sometimes you have to dismiss yourself from doubters in order to strengthen yourself in faith.

A seed can't grow just anywhere. Your soil matters. Your environment matters. Where you lay your head matters. Who you speak to on the phone matters. Because faith comes by hearing, what we hear often becomes what influences our lives.

One of my favorite Old Testament passages is when Israel marches around Jericho. However, Joshua makes a particular statement before the marching begins that always sticks out to me. He instructs everyone to be quiet until he tells them to shout (Josh. 6:10). He witnessed the power of negative words and their impact on people's faith when a generation refused to enter the Promised Land, and he wouldn't let them repeat that same mistake under his watch. He knew people create environments, and he refused to allow them to create a negative one.

Jesus modeled this, and we can follow His example. He didn't allow just anyone and everyone into His space. He loved everyone but was very protective of His environment. He sharply corrected His own disciple Peter when he spoke in ways that created an unhealthy environment. You must do the same. Find a community of believers who will strengthen you. Only then will your iron be sharpened by other iron.

Faith Fertilizer #4: Reflect on past experiences

It is impossible to have short memory and strong faith. Faith is strengthened when we remember past occasions where God revealed Himself. Our observation of previous experiences gives us the hope to believe again tomorrow.

In the Old Testament important episodes in Israel's faith journey were memorialized in and through altars, feasts, and memorials to remind them of God's faithfulness. Jesus even drew strength and faith from some of these stories. He often compared Himself with Jonah when He talked about His death and resurrection.

When you find yourself in a difficult situation and need your faith to be strengthened, realize the same God who moved mightily and faithfully on Israel's behalf is the same God you're serving right now. God has not changed. He is the same yesterday, today, and forever.

Rehearse His faithfulness in a prayer journal. Thank Him publicly and privately for every moment where His sovereign hand became obvious to you. You can find strength not just in the experiences of others but also in your own experiences. If you look back over your life, you will see overwhelming evidence of God's faithfulness. Those experiences can serve as fertilizers that will grow your faith.

It is in the strengthening of our faith that Christ is realized. It is when we remove ourselves from nonbiblical notions of faith that we can remind ourselves that faith is not about the reward but about knowing the God of the reward. Biblical faith infuses and empowers us to speak to the mountainous situations in our lives. Jesus said we would not only speak to mountains but also tell them where to go.

The faith Jesus demonstrated is much more achievable than you realize. I want to challenge you to search for it like children search for Waldo. Do not let the overwhelming crowd or the difficulty of the process cause your faith to wither away. If you want to be like Jesus...believe God.

Chapter 12

JESUS and the HOLY SPIRIT

Those in whom the Spirit comes to live are God's new Temple. They are, individually and corporately, places where heaven and earth meet.[1]
—N. T. WRIGHT

JESUS LIVED AN amazing, invigorating, and unforgettably impactful life. He is unequivocally the most influential person in human history. Thousands of years after His death, millions still trust Him with their lives. Those of us who have placed our faith in Him are intentionally attempting to live our lives like He did.

However, I think it's important for me to inform you: Jesus had some help. Yes, Jesus had help. He did not rely on His own innovation, ingenuity, or efforts to live His life or accomplish His assignment. He completely relied on a power beyond His human capability to empower and equip Him to be who He was and to do what He did.

He had the help of the Holy Spirit. He was born by the Spirit, baptized in the Spirit, anointed with the Spirit, and resurrected by the power of the Spirit. Every miracle

He performed was by the Spirit, and every temptation He overcame was made possible because of the Spirit. As a matter of fact, Jesus did nothing by Himself. John's Gospel says Jesus gave them this answer: "I tell you the truth, the Son can do nothing by himself. He does only what he sees the Father doing. Whatever the Father does, the Son also does" (John 5:19, NLT). His entire life was characterized by His reliance on the power of the Holy Spirit.

Just in case you aren't following my logic, if Jesus relied and depended on the Holy Spirit to *be* Jesus, then we also must rely and depend on the Holy Spirit to be *like* Jesus. We need the Spirit's help. I say this because not only does Scripture clearly communicate Jesus's dependence on the Holy Spirit, but Jesus also adamantly affirms our need for the Spirit as well. He makes it perfectly clear when talking to the disciples that in order to accomplish the mission He gives, we need the person, presence, and power of God the Holy Spirit.

This is the essence of the conversation He has throughout His entire ministry. His work was not complete until He went away to send the Holy Spirit. John 16:5–15 proves it:

> But now I am going to him who sent me. None of you asks me, "Where are you going?" Rather, you are filled with grief because I have said these things. But very truly I tell you, it is for your good that I am going away. Unless I go away, the Advocate will not come to you; but if I go, I will send him to you. When he comes, he will prove the world to be in the wrong about sin and righteousness and

judgment: about sin, because people do not believe in me; about righteousness, because I am going to the Father, where you can see me no longer; and about judgment, because the prince of this world now stands condemned.

I have much more to say to you, more than you can now bear. But when he, the Spirit of truth, comes, he will guide you into all the truth. He will not speak on his own; he will speak only what he hears, and he will tell you what is yet to come. He will glorify me because it is from me that he will receive what he will make known to you. All that belongs to the Father is mine. That is why I said the Spirit will receive from me what he will make known to you.

—JOHN 16:5–15

Look at this conversation closely. First, Jesus announces to His disciples that He has to leave and return to the Father. He knows this will upset them because for three years He has mentored, coached, and corrected them. But Jesus says in verse 7, "It is for your good"—or, it is for your advantage—"that I go away." If Jesus doesn't go away, the Holy Spirit can't come.

Jesus knew what the disciples did not know—that sometimes it is best for some things to leave so that other things can come. He knew they could not carry out the mission He would give them without having the power He relied upon to do His own work. Although they sat under His tutelage for three years, He knew information and education were not enough. He knew the Holy Spirit was so essential to their lives that He wouldn't allow them to do ministry until they had power. After

His resurrection, He returned to His disciples and said, "I am going to send you what my Father has promised; but stay in the city until you have been clothed with power from on high" (Luke 24:49). The Holy Spirit is well worth the wait, and Jesus knew if the Father promised them greater works, their waiting would not be in vain.

Perhaps you, like the disciples, are waiting for life to come together. Perhaps you are uncertain about why things haven't seemingly worked out yet. Could it be that you are trying to do life and ministry without power? Could it be that you have rushed ahead of God without waiting on the promise?

A third time Jesus addresses His disciples, but this time it is right before His ascension. Acts 1:4–5 records it like this:

> On one occasion, while he was eating with them, he gave them this command: "Do not leave Jerusalem, but wait for the gift my Father promised, which you have heard me speak about. For John baptized with water, but in a few days you will be baptized with the Holy Spirit."

Notice the trend of these conversations. Jesus seems to consistently repeat Himself. He says the same thing a few times and in different ways. He aggressively and intentionally emphasizes the importance of the Holy Spirit.

Now, if Jesus is this intentional about emphasizing this message, then it must be essential. The only way to do life and ministry Christ's way is to do it relying on the power of the Holy Spirit.

But How?

Thankfully the disciples obeyed Jesus and waited for the promise of the Spirit—and became people of power in doing so. But how do we become people of power? And if we already have the power of the Holy Spirit working in us, how do we experience Him in a greater way?

Practically speaking, I believe there are three fundamental steps we have to take. We must understand, embrace, and employ the Holy Spirit. These are the basic keys that will unlock the same power Jesus had. Let's look closely at all three.

Step #1: Understand the Holy Spirit

First, we must expand our understanding of the nature and identity of the Holy Spirit. I know many of you reading this book already know about the person, power, and presence of the Holy Spirit. However, just because we are aware of something doesn't mean we are aware of everything about it. There is always more we can learn because the nature and power of the Holy Spirit is limitless. Just like Christians need to be re-evangelized and retaught the gospel so they don't inadvertently end up in works righteousness, we also need to be reminded of the role of the Holy Spirit.

I know the idea of understanding the Holy Spirit sounds a bit complicated. When I say "understand Him," I mean have a working knowledge of what the Bible has to say about Him. For starters, you must know the Holy Spirit is the third person of the Trinity. The Holy Spirit is not an "it." The Holy Spirit is a He. As God, the Holy Spirit wants to indwell and infill us so He can transform us. I am not attempting to get into a theological

197

boxing match regarding the indwelling or the infilling of the Spirit. This book isn't about the person of the Holy Spirit, after all—it's a book about becoming more like Jesus, and this conversation about the Holy Spirit concerns the role He plays in that transformation. Therefore, my hope is that we will all understand that one of the primary roles of the Holy Spirit after regeneration is to make us like Jesus. This is the essence of sanctification. The Holy Spirit gives us all gifts, but that is not His primary role. He wants to make us like Jesus. One of the ways the Holy Spirit does this is by giving us an appetite for transformation. He produces a hunger for God that is necessary to experience our transformation into Christlikeness.

I need to ask you something: Are you hungry? I'm asking because I believe it's possible to be a Christian and not be hungry. There is an example of this with a group of believers in the early church:

> When the apostles in Jerusalem heard that Samaria had accepted the word of God, they sent Peter and John to Samaria. When they arrived, they prayed for the new believers there that they might receive the Holy Spirit, because the Holy Spirit had not yet come on any of them; they had simply been baptized in the name of the Lord Jesus. Then Peter and John placed their hands on them, and they received the Holy Spirit.
>
> —ACTS 8:14–17

Do you notice what happened here? Peter and John were sent to preach to believers. When they arrived, they prayed for them to receive the Holy Spirit. The apostles recognized the importance of the believers in Samaria understanding the significance of the Holy Spirit. If they were going to experience long-term, radical, Christlike transformation, it would only happen through their reliance on the Holy Spirit. Because of the Holy Spirit their cravings would change. They would gain an appetite for His presence like never before.

He works the same way for us. When you have the Spirit, you begin to have a "want to" in your spirit that pushes you to resist things in which you would've normally indulged. You have a desire to please God in public and private moments. You find yourself searching for truth, asking different questions, and accepting the will of God over the will of your wants—and your tree begins to produce fruit that resembles Jesus.

Step #2: Embrace the Holy Spirit

After you understand the Holy Spirit—and of course, you will never fully understand Him in totality!—you must embrace Him. If we have already embraced Him, then we should do it on another level. Imagine walking into a room, learning that the person standing in front of you is your long-lost sibling, and remaining distant from them. The first instinct we all would have would be to run to them, embrace them, and introduce ourselves. In the same way, when you rely on the Spirit, you run into the arms of God for guidance, protection, instruction, confession, relief, embrace, comfort, and a host of other needs. You soon come to realize the Holy Spirit was the best friend you've been searching for.

Ephesians 5:18 encourages us to "be filled with the Spirit." Not halfway, not partially, but fully. God intends for you to be filled with His Spirit such that your life overflows or spills over with God's presence. It's when Jesus simply overflows in every area of your life.

Being filled isn't necessarily about how much of the Spirit you have; it's really about how much of the Spirit has you. When this happens, everything changes. Your smile will hint at the fact that the Holy Spirit lives in you. Your tone of voice will change. Your sensitivity to people's needs and concerns will transform.

The Holy Spirit is the gift that keeps on giving. Refusing to embrace Him only leaves you like a kid on Christmas morning who has presents under the tree but refuses to open them.

At the same time, let me bring balance to this conversation. I'm sure certain segments of Christianity have made the Holy Spirit out to be some spooky, ghostlike cartoon. When He is mentioned in sermons, He's presented as a ghost that seduces people. He makes them roll on the floor and scream aloud. Hence, many people don't embrace the Holy Spirit because He has been misrepresented.

But you don't correct extremism by avoidance. I get it—some people are weird. However, just because some people are weird doesn't mean everything about the situation is wrong. Know this: everyone encounters the Spirit differently. Nevertheless, each of us should encounter Him, and we must rely on Him. Don't fight what you need.

Embrace that God is trying to take your hand so you can walk with Him into the next level of life. He wants to give you the power you've been yearning for in order to effectively do what Jesus did. Only the Holy Spirit will bridge the gap between the Jesus in our heads and the Jesus in the Bible, so don't run away from this holy invitation. Don't sabotage your future because of a preconceived notion. Ask the Lord to fill you with His Spirit, and resist the impulse to compare your experience to someone else's.

Step #3: Employ the Holy Spirit

After you understand the Holy Spirit and embrace Him for the God He is and not the caricature others have portrayed Him to be, you must then employ Him. In short, put Him to work. What do I mean? Fire you, and hire Him.

We all have this tendency to drift into works righteousness. It's a tendency that has been around since the days of the early church. Jesus dealt with it during His day too. The apostle Paul addressed it this way:

> You foolish Galatians! Who has bewitched you? Before your very eyes Jesus Christ was clearly portrayed as crucified. I would like to learn just one thing from you: Did you receive the Spirit by the works of the law, or by believing what you heard? Are you so foolish? After beginning by means of the Spirit, are you now trying to finish by means of the flesh?
>
> —GALATIANS 3:1–3

The Christians in Galatia were attempting to finish in their own strength what was started by the power of the Spirit. God started it, and God wants to finish it. You can't make up your mind that you're going to be like Jesus and accomplish it with will and effort. Actually, only Jesus can be like Jesus, and the Holy Spirit, which is the Spirit of Jesus, wants to be like Jesus through you. Your job is to surrender—to yield—and the Holy Spirit will work on you, in you, and through you to make you like Jesus.

It's great if you have amazing spiritual gifts. However, the apostle Paul says if you have gifts and don't have love, which is a character trait of Jesus, then you are just making noise. It's important to understand that the Holy Spirit's most important job is to work *on* us, not just *for* us.

If we give our will to God, the Spirit will do the work. If we fire ourselves and hire Him, God will enable us to benefit from the reward that submission and surrender bring. Employ the Spirit and you will see life in a totally different way. The Holy Spirit is our helper. He is our keeper and guide. If we are going to speak the truth in love, we need help. If we are going to love our enemies, we need help. If we are going to become people of grace and faith, we need help. In his book *Paul, the Spirit, and the People of God,* Gordon Fee says, "If the church is going to be effective in our postmodern world, we need to stop paying mere lip service to the Spirit and to recapture Paul's perspective: the Spirit as the experienced, empowering return of God's own personal presence in and among us, who enables us to live as a radically eschatological people in the present world while we await the consummation."[2]

Without the Holy Spirit we can do nothing. Don't end this re-presenting journey without stopping for a moment and asking yourself the question, "Do I have help that I'm not using?" If so, help is not just on the way. Help is here.

A FINAL WORD

WHEN YOU BEGAN this book, you began a journey of extreme spiritual significance. Our objective was to become Christians who are more like Christ, which at first seems like an unnecessary excursion and a redundant experience. Most of us would assume we, as Christians, are already like Christ. However, as we have seen, this is not always the case.

You agreed to take this ride with me through the Scriptures to make sure the Jesus of the Bible is consistent with the Jesus in your head and heart. We learned Jesus was a man of truth and we should be people of truth who tell the truth to God, ourselves, and others. We learned Jesus was a person of grace, and we should be people of grace who challenge without condemning and correct without condoning. We learned Jesus had mouth management, and we should manage our tongues as well.

In truth, the lessons we learned are too numerous to name. But after all the revelation has been shared and all of the cross-references have been made, what do we do with all of this? How do we apply these lessons in meaningful ways so our learning is not in vain? How do we reset our lives in order to re-present Christ in culture for the rest of our lives? I want to answer in the form of an acronym. In order to cement these chapters and lessons into your psyche and heart, you must allow God to KING you.

"KING ME"

When I was growing up, we often played checkers. If you're familiar with the game, you know that one of the vital strategies in checkers is to get kinged. When you get kinged, your chances of winning increase. As a result, your opponent has to pay close attention to your new reality, as you're able to move back and forth on the board with much greater freedom.

The same is true in a spiritual sense. When we get "kinged" in life by Jesus, we can advance more freely with our emotions, our resources, our marriages, and our jobs. But the only way we can do that is to understand three things. First, we have to know Jesus is King. Second, we have to acknowledge Him as King. Third, we have to live like we've been "kinged."

Step #1: Understand Jesus is King

At my church we have a frequent expression: "Jesus doesn't want to just save our lives. He wants to lead them." Never forget that. Jesus didn't enter the world only to die. He also came to show us how to live. He came so we would no longer have to be nomadic citizens in a foreign land without a trustworthy leader.

Now that we know Jesus, we know ourselves better. Now that we know Jesus, we no longer have to sit on the throne of our lives. Jesus is King. He is not just a way maker, but King. He is not just a problem solver, but King. He is not just a provider, but King. The Bible calls Him the King of kings and the Lord of lords. Therefore, if we are going to be better Christians, we have to first acknowledge Jesus as King.

If you were to travel to another country outside

America, you would recognize how different it is to live with a king. A monarch rules and reigns over the citizens of that particular place. Whatever the king says, goes. The king has no cabinet. The king needs no board or second opinions. When the king makes a decision, the people simply comply.

It's impossible to re-present Christ to the world if you haven't first understood Him to be King. Furthermore, Jesus wants to rule and reign in your life. He doesn't simply want to rescue you from bad habits and regrettable mistakes. He wants to completely reshape and reconstruct the way you understand yourself as a citizen of His kingdom in the earth. Which leads us to the second step...

Step #2: Acknowledge Jesus as your King

When a person has been kinged by Jesus, they not only understand Jesus *is* king, but they also make Him *their* king. Many individuals have unintentionally accepted Jesus as Savior but not acknowledged Him as Lord. They have not come to the place where they have made a concrete decision to let Jesus take the wheel.

When you acknowledge Jesus as your King, you decide, "From this point on, God's Word is going to have the final say over what I do with my life." That means, again, you have to fire yourself and hire Him. Your vote doesn't count. Your opinion doesn't matter. If the King says don't marry him or her, then you don't. If the King says forsake all and follow, then that's what you do.

In checkers, once you get kinged, it means another checker piece has been put on top of yours, and that gives you the ability to move with greater freedom around the board. In the same way, getting kinged by Jesus puts Him and His authority over you. He becomes your leader and your Lord. One of my mentors puts it this way: "When you get under what God has placed over you, you can get over what God has placed under you." When Jesus really gets over you—remember how submission was about coming under God's rule?—then you can get over the things in your life with greater ease.

Step #3: Live like you've been kinged

In checkers your experience of the game completely changes once you've been kinged. You can move more quickly and make more jumps than before. In the same way, being kinged by Jesus means living in a wholly new way. In fact, the word *king* forms an acronym for how we're meant to live. To live kinged by Jesus, you must *kneel, invite, notice,* and *guard.*

KNEEL, INVITE, NOTICE, GUARD

Kneel

Kneeling, or genuflecting, shows reverence and honor to the authority or power higher than you. We can't live kinged by Jesus if we don't kneel before Him. The only way we are going to be able to stand is if we make a decision to kneel. By kneel, I mean humble yourself, admit you are not your own boss, and commit to spending concentrated time with God. As we discussed in the disciplines chapter, you cannot do what Jesus did in public if you are not willing to live as Jesus lived in private. Your daily commitment to strengthening your spiritual life through prayer, worship, service, fasting, and reading the Scriptures is crucial to your overall kneeling posture.

Invite

When you've been kinged, you understand evangelism is not optional. It's mandatory. Evangelism is not something we engage in to acquire divine extra credit. It's fundamental to who we are. We want everyone to know the true King and serve Him also.

Jesus gives His disciples a word picture that communicates the urgency of evangelism in Luke 14:23, where He says, "Then the master told His servant, 'Go out to the roads and country lanes and make them come in, so that my house will be full.'"

This is our assignment. As Christians, we must witness. We must invite. We are not called to save others or die for them—that's Jesus's job! Since the hardest part has already been done, inviting people into it should be easy.

But the truth is, most of us get nervous about telling others about Jesus. However, when you're exposed to something good, it's impossible not to share it with others. When you finally see that movie others have recommended and it changes your perspective, you tell everyone you meet to go see it. That's just what the woman at the well did when she met Jesus:

> Then, leaving her water jar, the woman went back to the town and said to the people, "Come, see a man who told me everything I ever did. Could this be the Messiah?" They came out of the town and made their way toward him.
>
> —JOHN 4:28–30

The core of her evangelism can be summed up in two words: "Come see." She had been changed, and she wanted others to change. With one decision to leave her comfortable place, she eliminated every excuse one would give for evangelism. Leave it up to Christ to do the converting. You just have the conversation. The results are eternally rich and abundant. Look what happens after she opens her mouth to invite others to see Jesus:

> Many of the Samaritans from that town believed in him because of the woman's testimony, "He told me everything I ever did." So when the Samaritans came to him, they urged him to stay with them, and he stayed two days. And because of his words many more became believers.
>
> They said to the woman, "We no longer believe just because of what you said; now we have heard for ourselves, and we know that this man really is the Savior of the world."
>
> —JOHN 4:39–42

What if God wants to begin the next revival in you? What if God is going to use your "king me" status as a banner of love that will change your community forever? The woman spoke once, and the Samaritans in her town moved from secondhand knowledge to personal "king me" commitments. The challenge you have is to open your mouth and invite. Do not keep Jesus to yourself!

Notice

When you've been kinged, you notice the needs of others. You're no longer too busy to notice others' pain and misfortune. A kinged person asks the question, "Are you calling me to respond to this, God?"

An example of what it means to notice others is revealed in the story of the good Samaritan:

In reply Jesus said: "A man was going down from Jerusalem to Jericho, when he was attacked by robbers. They stripped him of his clothes, beat him and went away, leaving him half dead. A priest happened to be going down the same road, and when he saw the man, he passed by on the other side. So too, a Levite, when he came to the place and saw him, passed by on the other side. But a Samaritan, as he traveled, came where the man was; and when he saw him, he took pity on him. He went to him and bandaged his wounds, pouring on oil and wine. Then he put the man on his own donkey, brought him to an inn and took care of him. The next day he took out two denarii and gave them to the innkeeper. 'Look after him,' he said, 'and when I return, I will reimburse you for any extra expense you may have.'

"Which of these three do you think was a neighbor to the man who fell into the hands of robbers?"

The expert in the law replied, "The one who had mercy on him."

Jesus told him, "Go and do likewise."

—LUKE 10:30–37

Jesus ends the parable by telling His hearers—and that includes us—to go and do likewise. The command is clear. When we hear this passage, we cannot simply accept it as a great allegory or parable. Instead, we must use this knowledge to infuse our "notice ability." Christ has changed you so you can help someone else. When you live a life like that of Christ, you accept a life of divine interruptions. God will always drop someone into your life to make sure you notice their need and respond.

Guard

Lastly, when you've been kinged, you understand that embodying the gospel message is key to the message being transmitted. This means you have to guard yourself from weakness and poor behavior. These things are not only destructive for your own life, but also the body of Christ and its witness to the world.

You are God's ambassador. When you step into the community of Christ, you no longer represent yourself. You represent God. So guard your decisions and maintain your integrity. All of us have weaknesses. But when you have been kinged by Christ, you learn the importance of tending to and managing those weaknesses responsibly. Don't allow your life to be destroyed by them. Be strong in the Lord and in the power of His might.

Jesus gives strict warning about irresponsible living that causes others to stumble:

> If anyone causes one of these little ones—those who believe in me—to stumble, it would be better for them if a large millstone were hung around their neck and they were thrown into the sea. If your hand causes you to stumble, cut it off. It is better for you to enter life maimed than with two hands to go into hell, where the fire never goes out. And if your foot causes you to stumble, cut it off. It is better for you to enter life crippled than to have two feet and be thrown into hell. And if your eye causes you to stumble, pluck it out. It is better for you to enter the kingdom of God with one eye than

to have two eyes and be thrown into hell, where "the worms that eat them do not die, and the fire is not quenched." Everyone will be salted with fire.
—MARK 9:42–49

When Jesus says "cut off" and "pluck out," He's not speaking literally. He's telling us to take whatever steps we have to take in order to protect us from ourselves. Why? Because we want to make the family look good. We want to be individuals who bring glory, not shame, to God's family. We don't want to be like Judas. We want to be like Job, who made the family look good. We want to be like Joseph, who made the family look good. We want to be like Jesus, who made the family look *really* good.

A FINAL WORD

The purpose of this book isn't simply to encourage and instruct us to live like Jesus. It is also to encourage us to experience the life that Jesus gives. The kingdom of God is characterized by righteousness, peace, and joy (Rom. 14:17). The kingdom of God is the reign of the King or the "King's way." Therefore, when we live life the King's way, allowing the King to rule our lives from the throne of our hearts, then we will experience righteousness, peace, and joy. What I'm attempting to say is when we re-present Jesus, everyone benefits. We benefit and the world benefits.

The world needs Jesus. They need His love that secures them, His truth that sets them free, and His grace that gives them another chance. However, we are His representatives. We are His ambassadors in the world (2 Cor. 5:20). One of the ways the world will experience Him is through us! The questions we must ask ourselves are: "What Jesus am I representing?" "Am I representing the Jesus who is a concoction of tradition, my opinion, and a little truth?" "Or am I representing the Jesus of the Bible, the life-giving, direction-altering, and destiny-revealing Jesus?" It is the Jesus of the Bible who initiated something so powerful that it brought Rome to its knees. It is the Jesus of the Bible who took this insecure, lost, broken, and battered man who is writing to you and revolutionized his life. It's that Jesus who radically changed your life, and it is only that Jesus who will change the lives of others. The world needs Him as desperately as we need Him.

He, however, has been lost—lost in allegiances to political agendas, lost in folklore and tradition, lost in hate speech spewed in the name of a God those words don't reflect, lost in a liberalness that has mutated into lasciviousness. But you found the real Jesus. I found Him, and since I found Him I haven't been the same. Out of appreciation for what He has done to and through us, we have an obligation to re-introduce Him to others. As long as God gives me days and energy on this earth I will do everything I can to introduce as many as possible to Him by representing Him well. I believe you will do the same. When we do, it will be said of us what was said of the early church: these are they that turned the world upside down.

NOTES

INTRODUCTION

1. David Kinnaman and Gabe Lyons, *unChristian: What a New Generation Really Thinks About Christianity . . . and Why It Matters* (Grand Rapids, MI: Baker Books, 2007), 28.
2. Goodreads.com, "Mahatma Gandhi Quotes," http://www.goodreads.com/quotes/22155-i-like-your-christ-i-do-not-like-your-christians (accessed July 17, 2014).

CHAPTER 1: JESUS AND LOVE

1. EWTN Global Catholic Network, "Quotes of Mother Teresa," https://www.ewtn.com/motherteresa/words.htm (accessed June 25, 2014).

CHAPTER 2: JESUS AND TRUTH

1. Goodreads.com, "Herbert Agar Quotes," http://www.goodreads.com/quotes/40824-the-truth-that-makes-men-free-is-for-the-most (accessed June 25, 2014).
2. Goodreads.com, "Warren W. Wiersbe Quotes," http://www.goodreads.com/quotes/90554-truth-without-love-is-brutality-and-love-without-truth-is (accessed June 25, 2014).

CHAPTER 3: JESUS AND GRACE

1. BrainyQuote.com, "Friedrich Schiller," http://www.brainyquote.com/citation/quotes/quotes/f/friedrichs154941.html?ct=Friedrich+Schiller (accessed June 25, 2014).
2. Don Whitehead, *Attack on Terror: The FBI Against the Ku Klux Klan in Mississippi* (New York: Funk & Wagnalls, 1970), 4; as cited in Michael Frost and Alan Hirsch, *ReJesus: A Wild Messiah for a Missional Church* (Peabody, MA: Hendrickson Publishers, 2009), 1–2.
3. "Amazing Grace" by John Newton. Public domain.

CHAPTER 4: JESUS AND WISDOM

1. BrainyQuote.com, "Charles Spurgeon," http://www.brainyquote.com/quotes/quotes/c/charlesspu121393.html (accessed June 25, 2014).

CHAPTER 5: JESUS AND THE S-WORD

1. Wm. Paul Young, *The Shack: Where Tragedy Confronts Eternity* (Newbury Park, CA: Windblown Media, 2007).
2. Dallas Willard, *The Great Omission: Reclaiming Jesus's Essential Teachings on Discipleship* (New York: HarperOne, 2006), 14.

CHAPTER 6: JESUS AND GENEROSITY

1. Noah benShea, *Jacob the Baker: Gentle Wisdom For a Complicated World* (New York: Random House, 1989).
2. Patti Digh, *Life Is a Verb: 37 Days to Wake Up, Be Mindful, and Live Intentionally* (Guilford, CT: skirt!, 2008).

CHAPTER 7: JESUS AND SPIRITUAL DISCIPLINES

1. Goodreads.com, "Charles H. Spurgeon Quotes," http://www .goodreads.com/quotes/477961-i-must-take-care-above-all-that-i -cultivate-communion (accessed June 25, 2014).
2. Tony Evans, *Tony Evans Speaks Out on Fasting* (Chicago: Moody Publishers, 2000), 7.
3. Jentezen Franklin, *The Fasting Edge: Recover Your Passion. Recapture Your Dream. Restore Your Joy* (Lake Mary, FL: Charisma House, 2011), 206.

CHAPTER 8: JESUS AND RELATIONSHIPS

1. Tom Holladay, *The Relationship Principles of Jesus* (Grand Rapids, MI: Zondervan, 2008).
2. Dallas Willard, *Renovation of the Heart: Putting On the Character of Christ* (Colorado Springs, CO: NavPress, 2002), 105.

CHAPTER 9: JESUS AND WORDS

1. Robert Fulghum, *All I Really Need to Know I Learned in Kindergarten: Uncommon Thoughts on Common Things* (New York: Ballantine Books, 1988), 18.

CHAPTER 10: JESUS AND FORGIVENESS

1. Goodreads.com, "Hannah More Quotes," http://www.goodreads .com/quotes/234244-forgiveness-is-the-economy-of-the-heart -forgiveness-saves-the-expense (accessed June 25, 2014).
2. T. D. Jakes, *Let It Go: Forgive So You Can Be Forgiven* (New York: Atria, 2012).
3. Alfred Poirier, *The Peacemaking Pastor: A Biblical Guide to Resolving Church Conflict* (Grand Rapids, MI: Baker Books, 2006), 157.
4. Lewis B. Smedes, *Forgive and Forget: Healing the Hurts We Don't Deserve* (New York: HarperCollins, 1984).

CHAPTER 11: JESUS AND FAITH

1. Goodreads.com, "Thomas Aquinas Quotes," http://www.goodreads .com/quotes/344613-to-one-who-has-faith-no-explanation-is -necessary-to (accessed June 25, 2014).
2. Cyndi Stivers, "Up Against the Waldo," *Entertainment Weekly*, December 14, 1990.
3. Roy B. Zuck, John F. Walvoord, and Louis A. Barbieri Jr., *The Bible Knowledge Commentary: New Testament* (Colorado Springs, CO:

David C. Cook, 1983). Also, Mark 14:1 says it was Passover, which was held in the month of Nisan (April).

CHAPTER 12: JESUS AND THE HOLY SPIRIT

1. N. T. Wright, *Simply Christian: Why Christianity Makes Sense* (New York: HarperOne, 2006).
2. Gordon D. Fee, *Paul, the Spirit, and the People of God* (Peabody, MA: Hendrickson Publishers, 1996), xv.

PASSIO

PASSIONATE. AUTHENTIC. MISSIONAL.

Passio brings you books, e-books, and other media from innovative voices on topics from missional living to **A DEEPER RELATIONSHIP WITH GOD.**

Visit the Passio website for additional products and **TO SIGN UP FOR OUR FREE NEWSLETTER**

PASSIO
THE ART OF AUTHENTIC FAITH

WWW.PASSIOFAITH.COM
www.twitter.com/passiofaith | www.facebook.com/passiofaith

12771

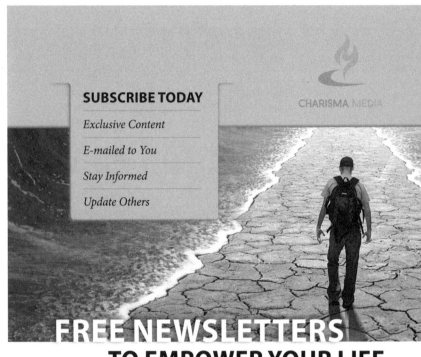